THE PLAY OF HEROD

A TWELFTH-CENTURY MUSICAL DRAMA

EDITED BY NOAH GREENBERG AND
WILLIAM L. SMOLDON

The Play of Herod

The Play of HEROD

A Twelfth-Century Musical Drama

EDITED BY
NOAH GREENBERG

AND
WILLIAM L. SMOLDON

Transcribed into modern musical notation
and translated into English by William L. Smoldon;
edited for modern performance by Noah Greenberg

New York   OXFORD UNIVERSITY PRESS   1965

© 1964, 1965 by Noah Greenberg and William L. Smoldon
Library of Congress Catalogue Card Number: 65-17430
All applications for permission to perform the play, whether admission is charged or not,
must be made in writing to the publishers:
Oxford University Press, Inc., 417 Fifth Avenue, New York, New York 10016.
Printed in the United States of America

Contents

Acknowledgments, vi

Introduction to the Performing Edition, vii

Summary of the Action, xiii

THE PLAY OF HEROD

Performing Edition, 3

Historical Notes, 75

Literal Transcription, 82

Notes on the Literal Transcription, 98

Acknowledgments

The frontispiece and other illustrative photographs are from the production of *The Play of Herod* as presented at The Cloisters, The Metropolitan Museum of Art, and are reproduced by kind permission of the Museum authorities.

The opening processional, "Orientis partibus", with the translation by Henry Copley Greene, is reprinted, by permission, from *Speculum*, VI, 4 (October 1931), published by the Mediaeval Academy of America.

The Play of Herod has been recorded by the New York Pro Musica and is available in the U.S.A. on Decca Records DXA 187 (Stereo DXSA 7187).

England: Brunswick Records
Australia: Decca Records

The editors gratefully acknowledge the advice and suggestions of Dr. Gustave Reese, Dom Anselm Hughes, The Benedictine Abbey of Solesmes, The Rev. James Kennedy O.S.C., Professor Jean Misrahi, and Charles C. Brown. They are especially thankful to Miss Margaret B. Freeman and The Cloisters staff who acted as artistic advisers to the original production. The editorial preparation and staging of *The Play of Herod* were aided by a grant from the Ford Foundation.

Text of the "Fleury play-book" (MS 201 of the Bibl. de Ville, Orléans) reproduced by kind permission of M. Claude Lannette, Conservateur aux Archives du Loiret.

Oxford University Press expresses its thanks to Messrs. Stainer and Bell of London, who published in 1960 an edition of *The Play of Herod*, also edited by W. L. Smoldon, and who have kindly assented to the publication of the present version.

Introduction to the Performing Edition

THE New York Pro Musica production of *The Play of Herod* was given its first performance at The Cloisters, The Metropolitan Museum of Art, in New York City in December 1963. The work in its present form (and this edition follows our performance as closely as possible) consists of two plays, *The Representation of Herod* and *The Slaying of the Children*, both from the twelfth-century French manuscript known as the "Fleury play-book." These works were written to appeal to a popular audience and were originally performed by the men and boys of the choir school attached to the monastic church of Fleury.

In our performance we added five musicians not mentioned in the manuscript: a percussionist, for the court of Herod, playing a tenor drum; a musician to Mary, who plays a bell carillon; and, for the Three Kings, three instrumentalists, who play a sopranino recorder, a tenor vielle, and a small bagpipe. Since the edition here is intended for practical use, we have substituted an oboe for the bagpipe and a modern viola for the tenor vielle. In addition to the music which appears in the manuscript we have interpolated an early processional song, the "Orientis partibus," two thirteenth-century French *estampies*, and, for the two crèche scenes, the thirteenth-century three-part motet, "Alleluya psallite." The plays were presented without an intermission and the running time is approximately one hour and fifteen minutes.

Inevitably one compares *The Play of Herod* with *The Play of Daniel*, since they are both French medieval works dating from roughly the same period, but one is struck by the great differences between them rather than the similarities. Dramatically and musically *Daniel* appears as a colorful processional drama in which all the players are brought to and from the staging area with joyous, dance-like, and sometimes forceful, processional music. The central hero figure of Daniel binds the different scenes together, and both his interpretation of the handwriting on the wall and the immensely moving lament sung in the lions' den stand in bold contrast to the rest of the piece. In *Herod*, however, we are given a series of highly contrasting scenes, each developing its own mood—the gentle naïveté of the exchange between the Midwives and Shepherds; the joyousness of the Three Kings; the dark character of the Herod court; the simple happiness of the adoration of the Magi. Then in even greater contrast the shocking slaying of the Innocents, followed by the long, almost resigned, lament of Rachel and her Consolers. Both works call for the singing of the Te Deum and it is interesting to compare the sound of the Te Deum after each. At the end of *Daniel* the Te Deum seems to sound like a song of celebration for the triumph of good over evil, but following the slaying of the children the Te Deum comes as balm and brings with it great relief from tragedy.

The Play of Herod does contain a few dance-like processional pieces (numbers 15 and 47, for example), and these are quite appropriately assigned to the Magi, but much of the music consists of fragments of chant for "recitative," and it borrows a large number of older liturgical antiphons which appear throughout. These pieces must have been very well known in the twelfth century because the original manuscript gives only the openings ("incipits") of these religious songs.

The stage director for the New York Pro Musica production, Nikos Psacharopoulos, and the designer, Rouben Ter-Arutunian, arranged the stage area in the chancel in such a way that the court of Herod occupied stage right. This area was dominated by a raised throne and a long platform running diagonally toward downstage center. The Manger occupied up-stage center and was much higher than the throne. Encircling the sides and back of the Manger was a set of steps built for the Angel Choir, and the Archangel appeared on a platform above the Manger. The down-stage left area was reserved for the Shepherds in the field and the appearances in the chancel of the Three Kings. The slaying of the Innocents and the lament of Rachel were staged in the front center area.

It is extremely fortunate that many of the liturgical dramas that have survived contain a great number of stage instructions, and I think it is important that the stage director be as faithful to these rubrics as the musical director should be with the notation. The rubrics in *Herod* were an enormous help in preparing the play, telling us much about the medieval performance, the attitudes of the actors, the costuming, and the general spirit of the play. References like the

"joyful" singing of the Innocents on their first appearance even give us clues about the interpretation of the music.

There is, of course, no *one* way to present a work such as *Herod*. The New York Pro Musica Cloisters performance should not be thought of as a definitive presentation, but rather as one possible approach.

The present edition attempts to reconstruct the 1963 performance, making certain concessions to practicality. The Shepherds in the Cloisters performances were sung by countertenors (male altos). These roles could easily be performed by female altos and are so assigned here. I have already listed the substitution of modern for old instruments above. The original stage instructions are printed, in literal translation, throughout, and additional suggestions for staging appear in italics. The suggested repetitions of certain sections, which we found necessary for our own production, are of course optional, as are the interpolated sections.

The doubling of certain roles is suggested here, but this depends entirely on the number of performers available. Only two very fast costume changes are involved: the Angel Choir becoming the Innocents and the Second King changing into Joseph. The other suggested doublings are the Midwives and Shepherds changing into Mothers-Consolers; and the First and Third Kings, Scribes, and Courtiers becoming Soldiers for the slaying scene. However, if the director has a large number of players at his disposal, doubling becomes unnecessary.

It is also possible to combine certain roles. Aside from the Angel Choir, the manuscript refers to a number of Angels, but in our performance we found it more practical to use an Archangel, who remains at his station above the Manger throughout the entire play. Although it is not absolutely clear, the manuscript seems to call for Spokesmen (or Interpreters) as well as two young Courtiers "dressed as young men" in the Herod court, but these are very small parts indeed and we combined the roles of Courtier and Spokesmen. For school productions it might be useful to have different children play the roles of Angels and Holy Innocents. Apparently, both Mothers of the Innocents and Consolers to Rachel were used in the twelfth-century production, but here again we found it more practical to combine these roles. Thus in *The Slaying of the Children* at number 13, the Mothers of the Children come on to intercede with the slayers and during the lament of Rachel these Mothers become Rachel's Consolers. Again, many directors might prefer not to combine these roles.

The bell carillon, played by the Musician to Mary, has an extremely important role in our production. In some of the processional pieces, the bells were used as hand-bells, but through most of the play they were mounted on a specially constructed wooden rack and hung in sequence so that they could give pitches to the performers and accompany a good deal of the singing. The bells were struck with leather mallets and were hung in the following order:

The only major stage properties are the curtained Manger with its surrounding steps for the Angel Choir, and Herod's throne, which stands on a platform extending from downstage right toward stage center. The smaller properties include:

a star mounted on a long pole

a medallion, again mounted on a pole, depicting the Lamb of God carrying a cross (an alternative to the medallion would be a banner)

swords for Herod, Archelaus, Armiger, and the Soldiers of the court

a scepter for Herod

a large book for the Scribes

staffs for the Shepherds

three gifts and three pillows for the Bearers of the Three Kings

a doll wrapped in swaddling clothes to represent the Christ-child

a coverlet for the Magi

As regards costuming, the basic guide should be the many medieval depictions of this very famous story. There are hundreds of such examples from twelfth- and thirteenth-century art which will serve better than any description.

NOAH GREENBERG

Summary of the Action

THE REPRESENTATION OF HEROD

"When Herod and the other persons are ready, an Angel shall appear with a multitude of the heavenly host. Seeing this, the shepherds are sore afraid. He shall announce salvation unto them, while the rest keep silent." Thus begins *The Play of Herod* according to the rubric in the "Fleury play-book." Then follows the journey of the shepherds to Bethlehem and their adoration of the Christ-child. The dialogue at the Manger is between the Shepherds and two Midwives, who, according to the apocryphal gospels, were present at the scene of the Nativity. After the Shepherds have worshipped the Child, they invite the audience to adore him also.

Meanwhile the Magi approach from three separate parts of the church as if they came from three different countries. The Magi greet each other, behold the Star, and proceed to Jerusalem, led by the Star.

At this point King Herod's court comes into action. Herod sends his armor-bearer (Armiger) and then his courtiers to inquire of the Magi who they are and what their purpose is. When the Magi are conducted to Herod they are again questioned, this time by Herod himself. The Magi explain that they have come from the East to seek a new-born King. Hearing this, Herod commands his Scribes "who are ready with their beards" to search in their books for a prophecy of such a King. The Scribes, turning over the pages for a long time, hand their book to Herod, pointing with a finger to the prophecy. Herod is seized with fury, and throws down the book; but his son, Archelaus, "comes forward to appease his father." And so Herod sends forth the Magi to search for the new-born King and bids them return to him with news of the Child.

The Magi, again following the Star, proceed toward Bethlehem, and on the way they meet and converse with the Shepherds returning from the Manger. As was the case with the Shepherds, the Magi speak with the Midwives at the Manger, and then offer their gifts to the Child. This done, they fall asleep and are warned by the Angel in a dream to return home another way. The Magi depart, avoiding King Herod's court.

THE SLAYING OF THE CHILDREN

The Slaying of the Children begins with the entrance of the young boys, the Innocents, in white garments, who later follow the symbolic Lamb bearing a cross.

Meanwhile Herod ceremoniously receives his scepter from Armiger, his armor-bearer.

At this point the Angel warns Joseph to flee into Egypt, for Herod would seek the Child to destroy him. And so the Holy Family departs, Mary carrying her son.

Then Armiger announces to Herod that the Magi have journeyed home another way. This

so angers Herod that he seizes his sword and is about to kill himself when Armiger suggests that he slay all the young boys instead, for perhaps "among them is found the Christ." So the Children are put to the sword while the Mothers try in vain to prevent the massacre. Rachel, one of the Mothers, sings a long lament while Consolers attempt to ease her sorrow. This scene is developed from the prophecy of Jeremiah quoted in the gospel of Matthew: "A voice in Rama was heard, lamentation and great mourning; Rachel bewailing her children, and would not be comforted, because they are not." After Rachel has been conducted from the scene, the Angel sings "Suffer the little children to come unto me"; and at the voice of the Angel, the Children "rise up and enter the choir singing."

Now Herod dies and his son Archelaus rules in his place.

In the final scene the Angel announces to Joseph that it is safe to "come out of Egypt" because Herod is dead, and the Holy Family returns into Galilee, Joseph singing "Gaude, gaude, gaude."

The cantor begins the Te Deum and the play ends.

MARGARET B. FREEMAN
THE CLOISTERS
METROPOLITAN MUSEUM OF ART
NEW YORK CITY

The Play of Herod

PERFORMING EDITION

Characters

Solo voices

Archangel	TENOR
Two Midwives	SOPRANOS
Three Magi	BARITONES
Armiger	BASS
Herod	BASS
Archelaus, Herod's Son	BASS
Two Courtiers	TENORS
Two Scribes	TENORS
Joseph	BARITONE
Rachel	MEZZO SOPRANO

Choir*

Angel Choir	TEN SOPRANOS
Three Shepherds	THREE ALTOS
Holy Innocents	TEN SOPRANOS
Soldiers	SIX BARITONES AND/OR TENORS
Mothers-Consolers	FIVE SOPRANOS AND/OR ALTOS

Instrumentalists

Musician to Mary	BELL CARILLON
Musicians to the Magi	SOPRANINO RECORDER
	VIOLA
	OBOE
Musician to Herod	TENOR DRUM

Actors

Virgin Mary	A YOUNG WOMAN
Star Bearer	A CHILD
Two Soldiers	TWO MEN
Three Gift Bearers	THREE CHILDREN

* The size of the choir may vary

The Representation of Herod

OPENING PROCESSIONAL

* *When Mary and the Child are ready behind the drawn curtains of the Manger and the Three Kings have taken their positions at the rear of the nave, the Archangel prepares to ascend the steps leading to his place above the Manger at the sound of the bells.*

The following members of the cast, in the order listed, enter from the rear of the nave and proceed down the center aisle singing "Orientis partibus."

Musician to Mary (Bells g¹ and d¹), Star Bearer, Angel Choir, Midwives, Shepherds, Courtiers, Scribes, Herod, Archelaus, Armiger

1. O - ri - en - tis par - ti - bus   Ad - ven - ta - vit a - si - nus,
   Out from the lands of Orient   Was the Ass divinely sent

2. Hic in col - li - bus Si - chan   Iam nu - tri - tus sub Ru - ben,
   In the hills of Sichem bred,   Under Reuben nourished,

3. Sal - tu vin - cit hin - nu - los,   Dam - mas et cap - re - o - los,
   Higher leap'd than goats can bound,   Doe and roebuck circled round;

4. Au - rum de A - ra - bi - a,   Thus et myr - rham de Sa - ba
   Red gold from Arabia,   Frankincense and from Sheba

5. Dum tra - hit ve - hi - cu - la,   Mul - ta cum sar - cin - u - la
   While he drags long carriages,   Loaded down with baggages,

6. Cum a - ris - tis or - de - um   Co - me - dit et car - du - um:
   Chews the ears with barleycorn   Thistledown with thistlecorn.

7. A - men di - cas, a - si - ne,   Iam sa - tur de gra - mi - ne
   Stuff'd with grass, yet speak and say   Amen, ass, with ev'ry bray:

**Stage directions appearing as rubrics in the original manuscript are printed in* roman. *Editorial additions are printed in italic.*

1. Pul-cher et for- tis-si-mus, Sar-ci-nis ap- tis-si-mus.
   Strong and very fair was he, Bearing burdens gallantly.
2. Tran-si-it per Ior-da-nem, Sa-li-it in Beth-le-em.
   Jordan's stream he traversed, Into Bethlehem he sped.
3. Su-per dro-me-da-ri-os Ve-lox Ma-di-a-ne-os.
   Median dromedaries' speed, Overcame and took the lead.
4. Tu-lit in ec-cle-si-a Vir-tus A-si-na-ri-a.
   Myrrh he brought and, through the door, Into the church he bravely bore.
5. Il-li-us man-di-bu-la Du-ra-te-rit pa-bu-la
   He, with jaws insatiate, Fodder hard doth masticate.
6. Tri-ti-cum e pa-le-a Se-gre-gat in a-re-a
   On the threshing floor his feet Separate the chaff from wheat.
7. A-men, A-men, i-te-ra, As-per-na-re ve-te-ra
   Amen; Amen, say again; Ancient sins hold in disdain.

1.-7. Hez, sir as-ne, hez!
     Heigh, Sir Ass, oh heigh!

(If the length of the nave requires it, some of the verses may be repeated.)

At the conclusion of the procession, the Angel Choir has taken its place above the Manger and the Star Bearer stands to one side near the Angels. The Midwives station themselves at the foot of the Manger and the Shepherds occupy down-stage left. Herod and his court briefly take their places and then leave by up-stage right before the end of the processional.

SCENE I ANGELS AND SHEPHERDS

At the sound of the bell preceding "Nolite timere vos," the Shepherds turn with fear, looking up to the Archangel.

Here begins the Book of the Representation, "Herod." Herod and the other members of the cast being ready to go on, then let the Angel appear above with a multitude of other Angels. Seeing this, the Shepherds are afraid. While the other Angels still remain silent, let the Angels sing greetings:

And thus let them proceed as far as the Manger which has been prepared at the monastery doors, and then let two women guarding the Manger question the Shepherds, saying:

Let the Shepherds reply:

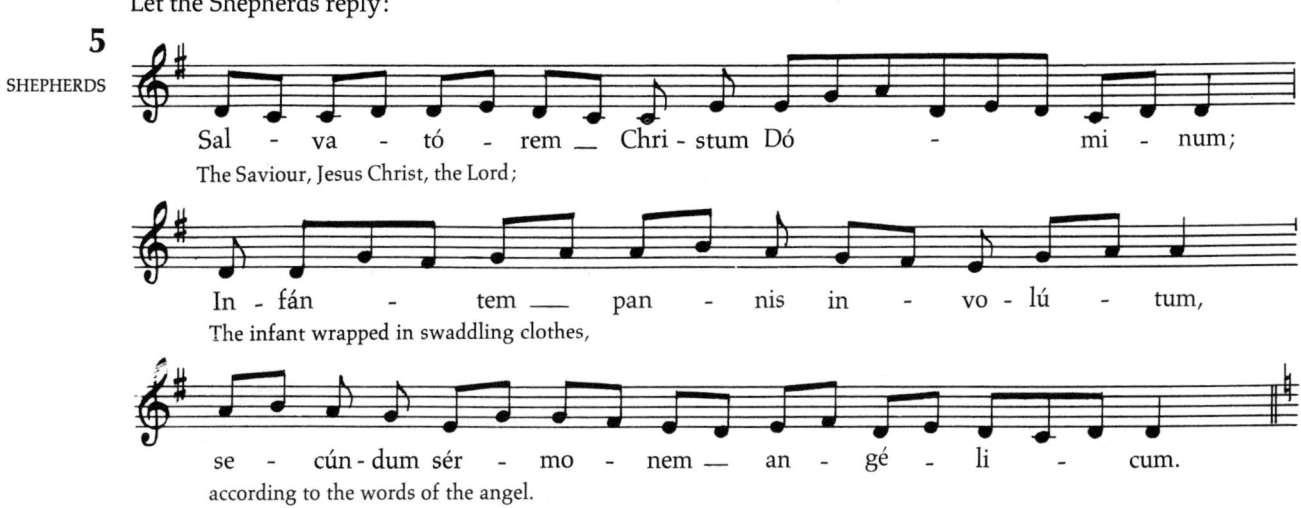

The women:

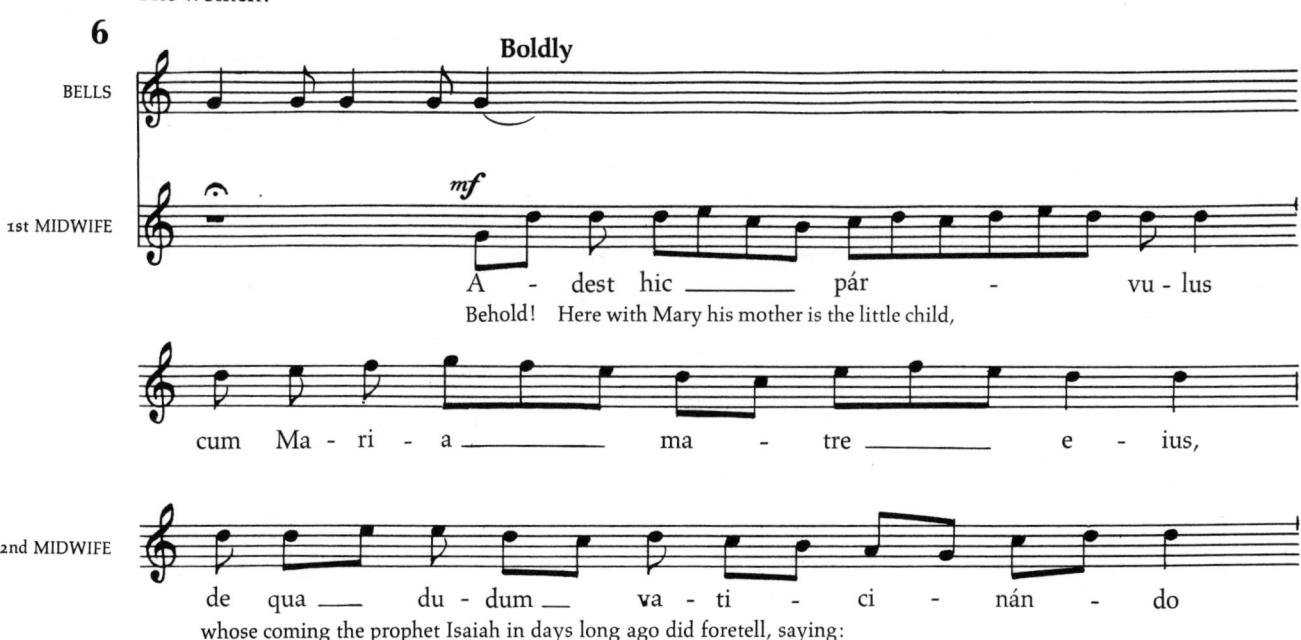

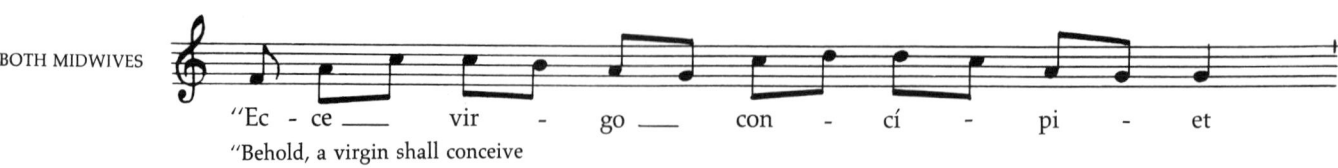

"Behold, a virgin shall conceive

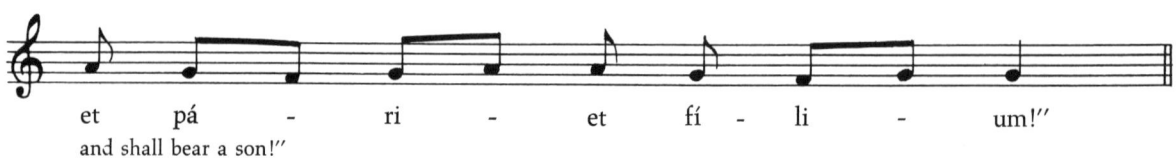

and shall bear a son!"

The Midwives slowly open the curtains of the Manger, showing Mary and the Child, and then close them at the end of the following motet.

6a **Delicately in moderate tempo**

Then let the Shepherds, prostrating themselves, adore the Child saying:

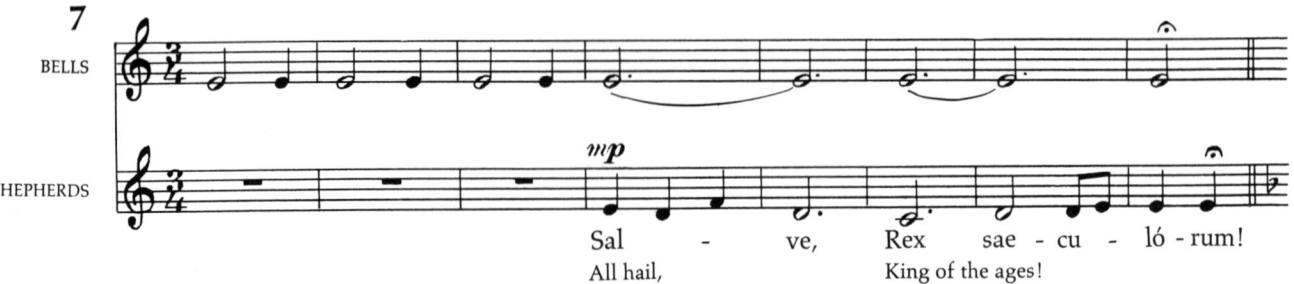

Then rising, let them invite the people around to worship the Infant,
saying to the crowd near by:

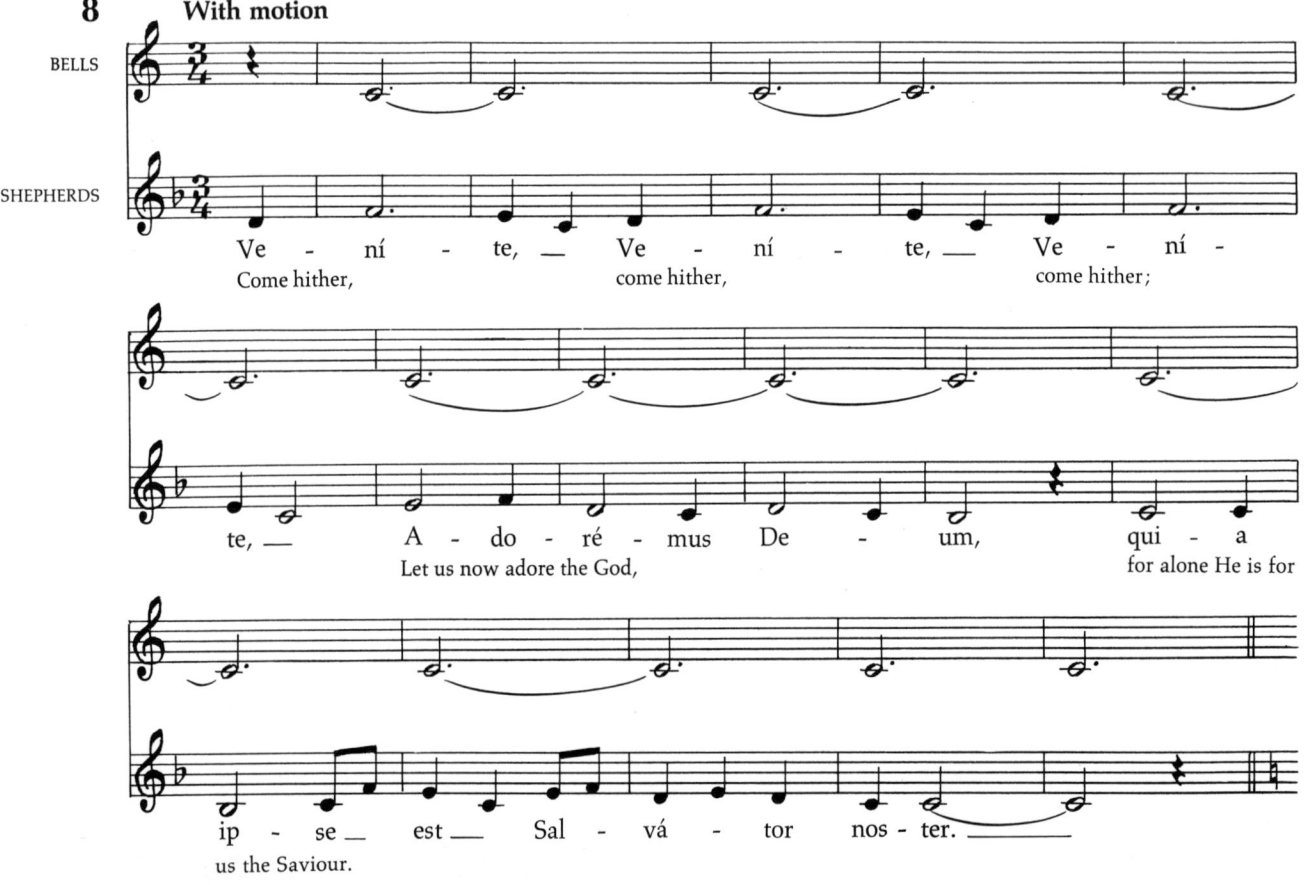

The Shepherds retire to up-stage left.

The Three Kings, each with Musician and Gift Bearer, stand ready at the rear of the nave as follows:

Right Aisle—1st King with Recorder Player and Gift Bearer
Center Aisle—2nd King with Oboe Player and Gift Bearer
Left Aisle—3rd King with Viola Player and Gift Bearer

Musicians began their estampie while walking a few steps into the nave, returning to follow their Kings when they begin to sing. The Magi procession should be timed so that the Three Kings meet on the steps leading to the center of the stage or chancel.

SCENE II THE THREE KINGS

Meanwhile, let the Magi advance, each coming from his own corner as if from his own region, meeting before the altar, or at the place of the Star, and while they are approaching, let the 1st say:

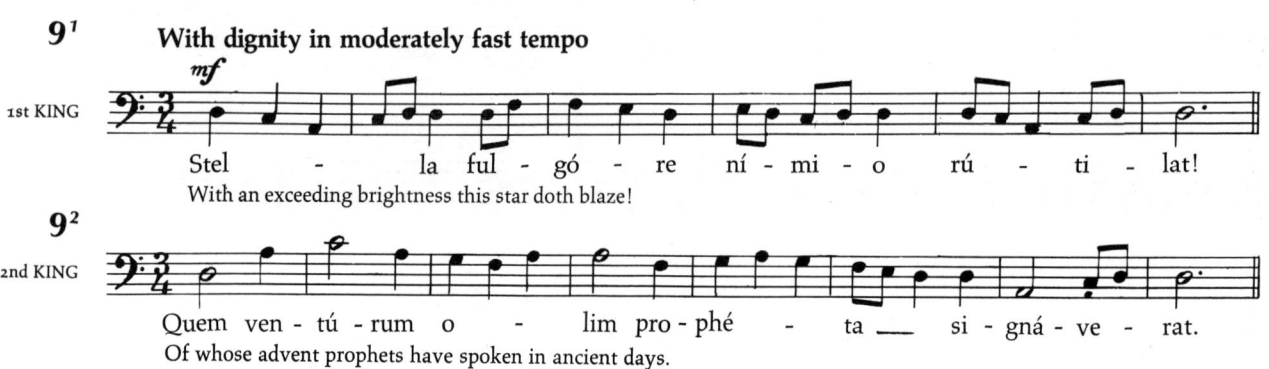

Then standing side by side, let him on the right hand say to the one in the middle:

10¹

3rd KING: Pax tibi, frater!
Peace to you, O brother!

And let the other reply:

10²

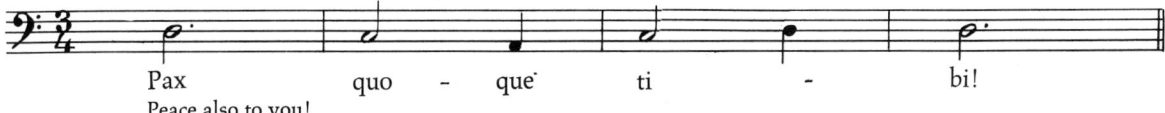

1st KING: Pax quoque tibi!
Peace also to you!

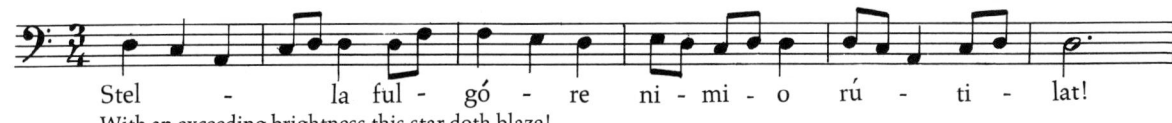

3 KINGS: Stella fulgóre nimio rútilat!
With an exceeding brightness this star doth blaze!

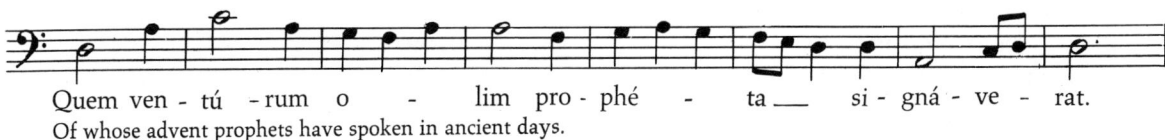

Quem ventúrum olim prophéta signáverat.
Of whose advent prophets have spoken in ancient days.

Pax tibi, frater! Pax quoque tibi!
Peace to you, O brother! Peace also to you!

(Accompanying the Kiss of Peace)

10a

RECORDER

VIOLA

Then let them kiss each other thus:

The middle to the left and the left to the right—a salutation to each one *(therefore it would seem the middle to the right also)*. Then let them indicate the Star to each other.

As the Kings kiss and then sing "Ecce Stella," the three Musicians stand to one side and the three Bearers to the other.

The Kings, Bearers, and Musicians are slowly led to down-stage left. The Star then advancing and leading them, let them follow saying:

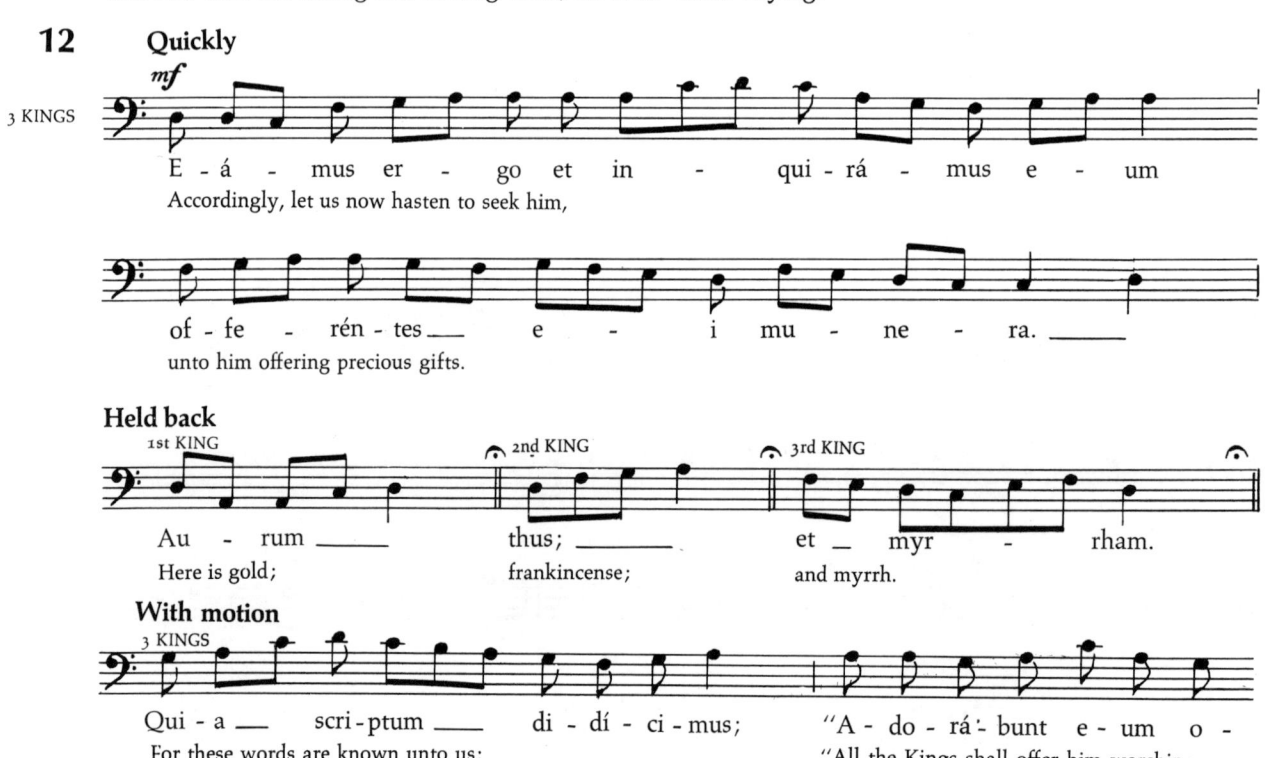

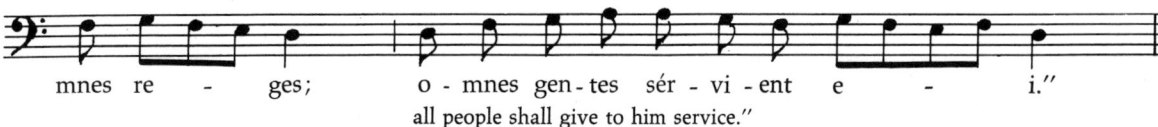

Coming to the choir door, let them question those standing by:

13   Deliberately

3 KINGS

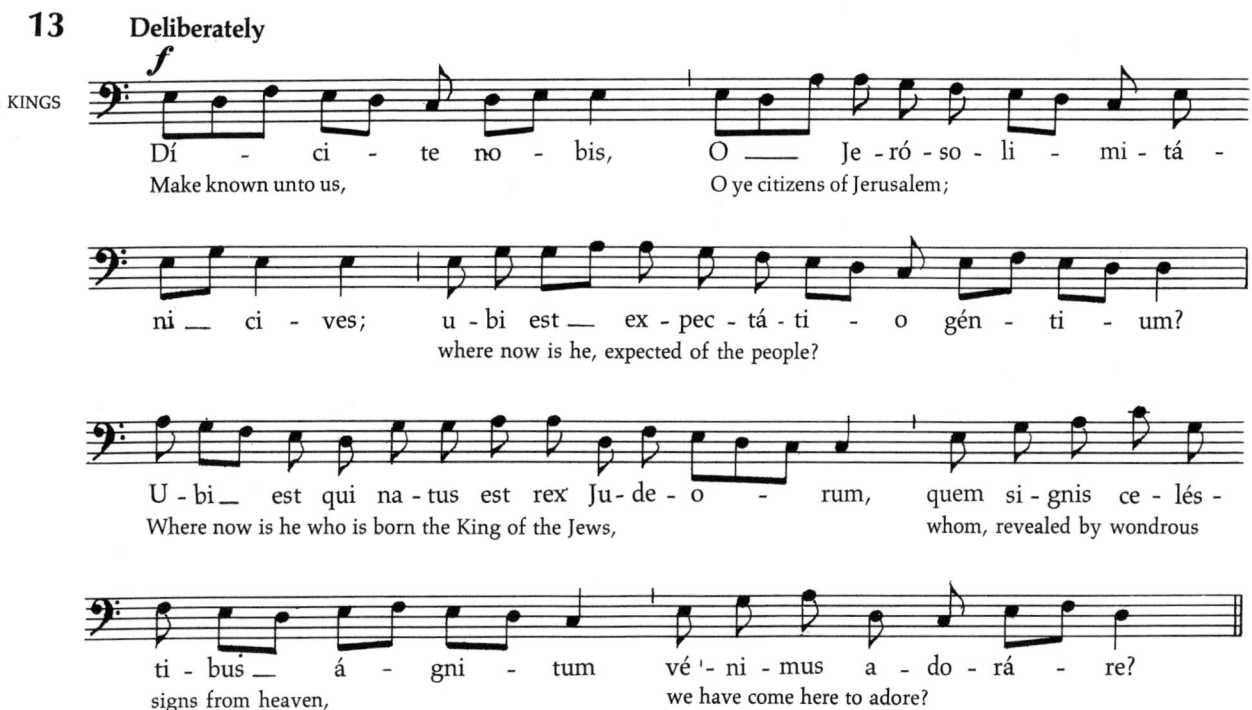

While the estampie is being played Herod enters with Archelaus, the Armiger, his Musician, two Courtiers, and two Soldiers. They all take their places in the throne area.

13a   Brightly (in one)

SCENE III HEROD'S COURT

Having seen them, let Herod send the Armiger to them, who says:

14 Forcefully

ARMIGER: Quae rerum nóvitas, aut quae causa subégit vos ignótas temptáre vias? Quo ténditis ergo? Quod genus? Unde domo? Pacem ne huc fertis an arma?

What unwonted events, or what reason moved you thus to attempt an unknown journey? Where, then, are you going? What race are you? Where is your home? Which do you bring to us, peace or war?

The reply of the Magi:

15 With joyous dignity, moderately fast

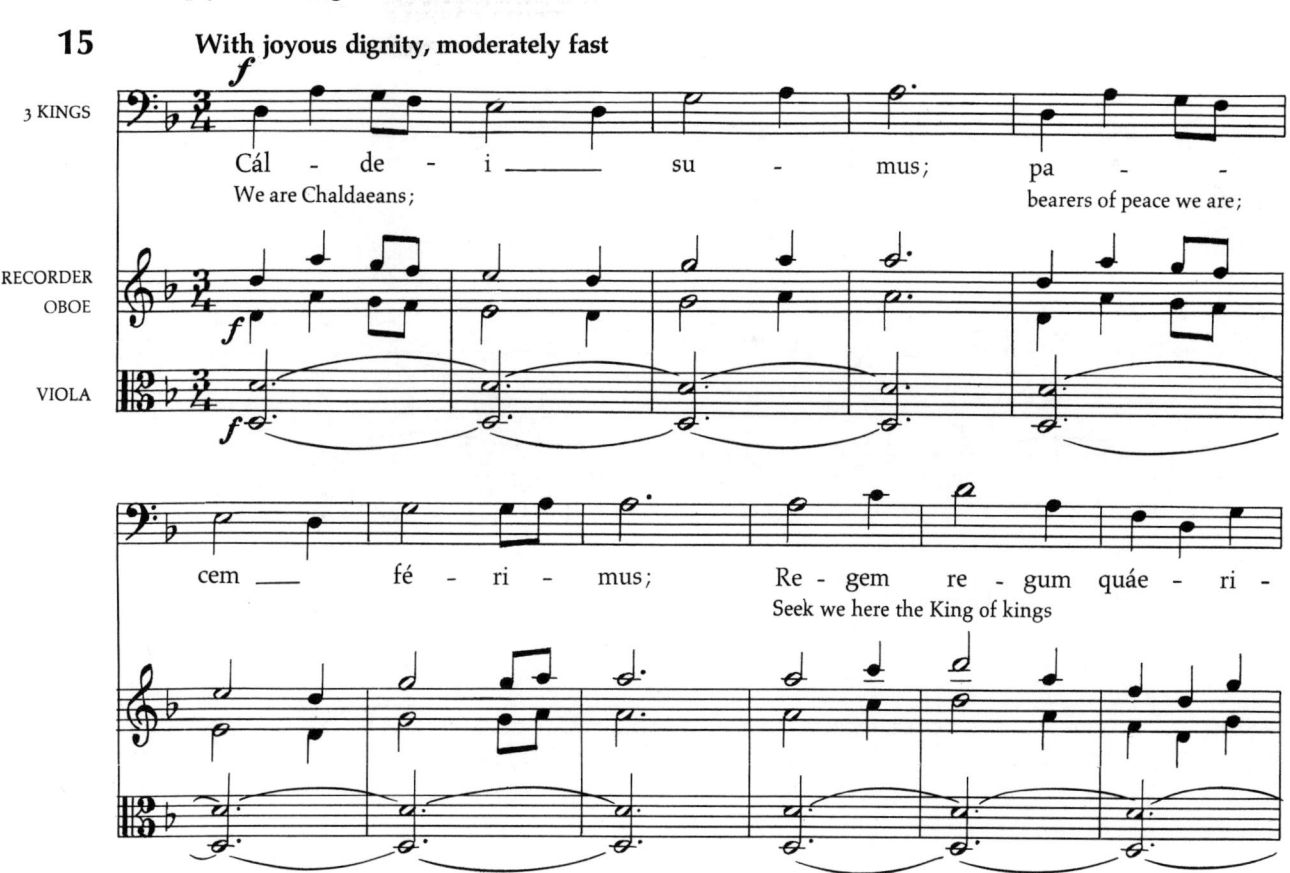

3 KINGS: Cáldei sumus; pacem férimus; Regem regum quaerimus

We are Chaldaeans; bearers of peace we are; Seek we here the King of kings

mus, quem natum esse stella indicat, quae
Whose birth is now revealed by the Star,
The

fúlgore céteris clárior
shining of which has exceeded all others in brightness.

rútilat.

The Armiger returns and salutes the King:
On bended knee let him say:

16
ARMIGER

Vivat Rex in aetérnum!
Live for ever, O King!

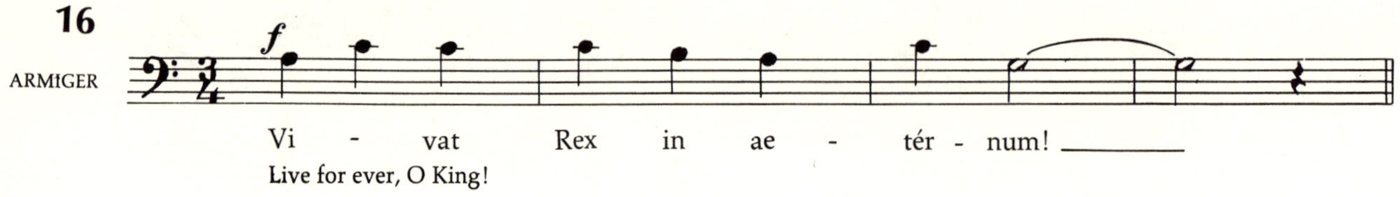

Armiger to the King:

Then let Herod send his Spokesmen or Interpreters *(Courtiers)* to the Magi, saying:

While beckoning and leading the Courtiers to the Magi the Armiger sings:

19a

ARMIGER

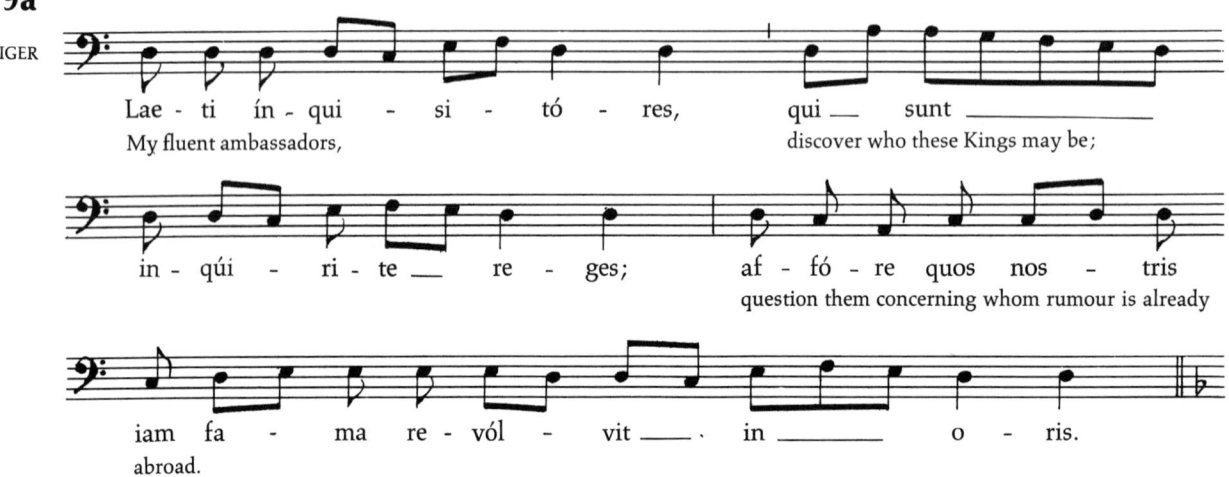

The Interpreters (Courtiers) to the Magi:

20

2 COURTIERS

The Magi:

21

3 KINGS

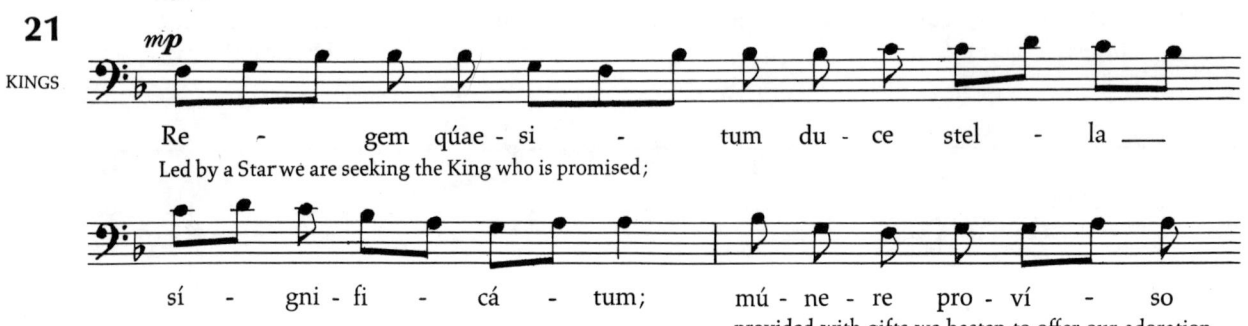

The Spokesmen *(Courtiers)* returning to Herod:

22 2 COURTIERS

Re - ges sunt Á - ra - bum; cum tri - no mú - ne - re; Na - tum quae - runt in - fán - tem, quem mon - strant sí - de - ra re - gem.
Kings of Araby are they; bringing a threefold gift; seeking a new-born infant, whom the stars proclaim to be King.

The Armiger to Herod:

22a ARMIGER

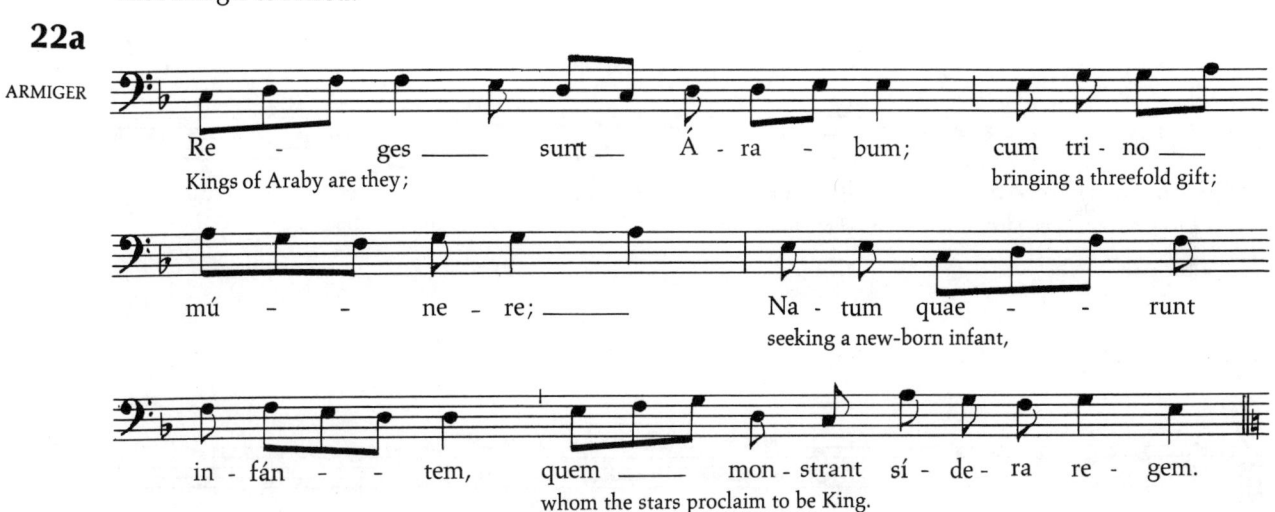

Re - ges sunt Á - ra - bum; cum tri - no mú - ne - re; Na - tum quae - runt in - fán - tem, quem mon - strant sí - de - ra re - gem.
Kings of Araby are they; bringing a threefold gift; seeking a new-born infant, whom the stars proclaim to be King.

Herod, sending the Armiger to bring the Magi:

23 DRUM / HEROD

An - te ve - ní - re iu - be,
Order them to attend us,

quo pos-sim sín-gu-la sci-re qui sunt;
that we may learn each of these things; who they are;

cur vé-ni- ant; quo nos
whence they have come; what rumour has brought them to us?

ru-mó - - re re-quí-rant?

Armiger:

24
ARMIGER

Quod man-das, cí-ti-us, Rex in-cli-te, per-fi-ci-é-tur.
What you have commanded, O famous King, swiftly shall be done.

The Armiger returns to the Magi while the court sings.

24a
2 COURTIERS

Quod man-das, cí-ti-us, Rex in-cli-te, per-fi-ci-é-tur.
What you have commanded, O famous King, swiftly shall be done.

The Armiger to the Magi:

25 **Forcefully**
ARMIGER

Ré - gi-a vos man-dá-ta vo-cant; non sé-gni-ter i-te!
You are summoned by the King's command; Come now without delay!

The Armiger, leading the Magi to Herod:

Herod to the Magi:

27 **With arrogance**

HEROD

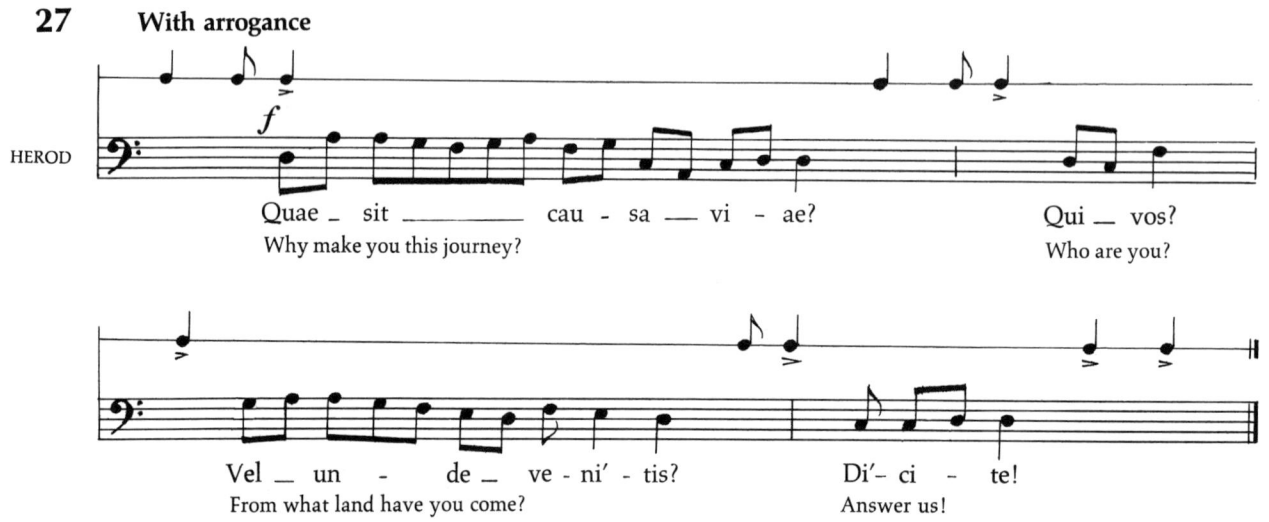

Quae _ sit _ cau - sa _ vi - ae?
Why make you this journey?

Qui _ vos?
Who are you?

Vel _ un - de _ ve - ni' - tis?
From what land have you come?

Di' - ci - te!
Answer us!

The Magi:

28 **Calmly**

3 KINGS

Rex _ est _ cau - sa _ vi - ae; Re - ges _ su - mus ex _ A - rá - bi - tis, huc _ ve - ni - én - tes.
The reason is a King; Kings are we, come from Arabia, journeying hither.

Quáe - ri - mus en _ re - gem re - gnán - ti - bus im - pe - ri - tán - tem;
Behold, we are seeking a king who rules all other rulers;

Quem na - tum _ mun - do lac - tat Ju - dá - i - ca vir - - - go.
who, newly born, is suckled by a Jewish virgin.

24

The Magi:

Then let them display the gifts. Let the First say:

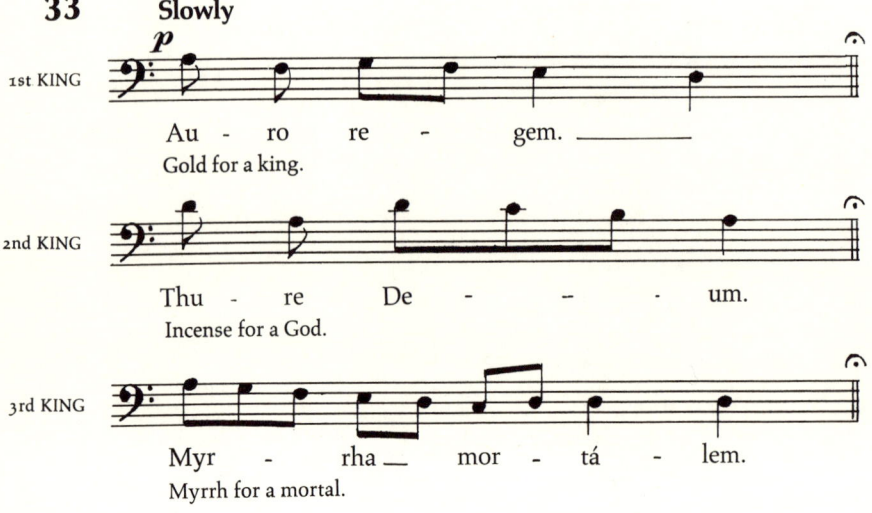

Then let Herod command the Courtiers, who are seated with him dressed as young men, to bring the Scribes, who, bearded, are near at hand:

34 **Bursting in**

Vos meí Symmýstae Legis perítos ascíte ut discant in Prophétis quid séntiant ex his.
You, O my courtiers, summon those learned in the law; let them say what they find in the prophets as to this.

The Courtiers to the Scribes, who are bringing with them the Books of the Prophets:

35

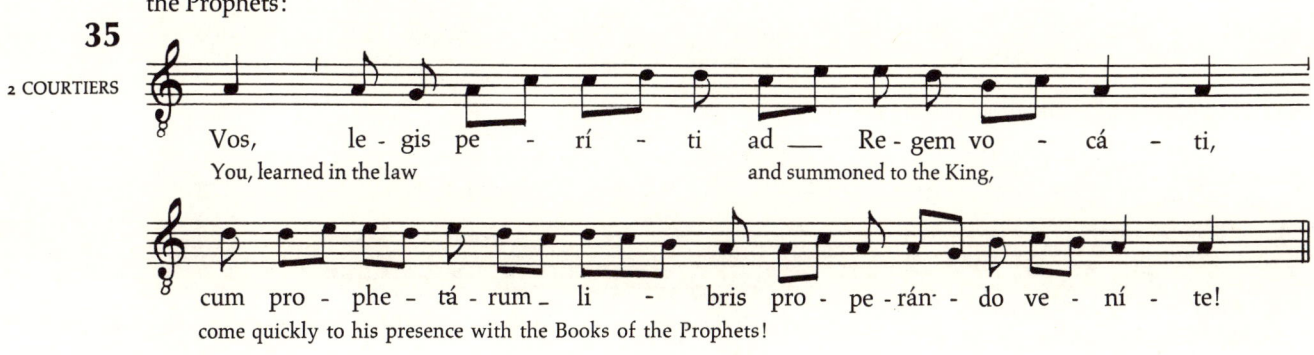

2 COURTIERS

Vos, legis períti ad Regem vocáti, cum prophetárum libris properándo veníte!
You, learned in the law and summoned to the King, come quickly to his presence with the Books of the Prophets!

Then let Herod question the Scribes, saying:

36

O vos Scribae; interrogáti
Hear us, you Scribes; we request you to inform us

dí - ci - te si quid de hoc pu - e - ro scri -
if you see anything written in the book concerning this boy.

ptum vi - dé - ri - tis in li - bro.

Then let two Scribes turn the pages, and finally, as if having discovered the prophecy, let them say:

37 **Slow**
2 SCRIBES

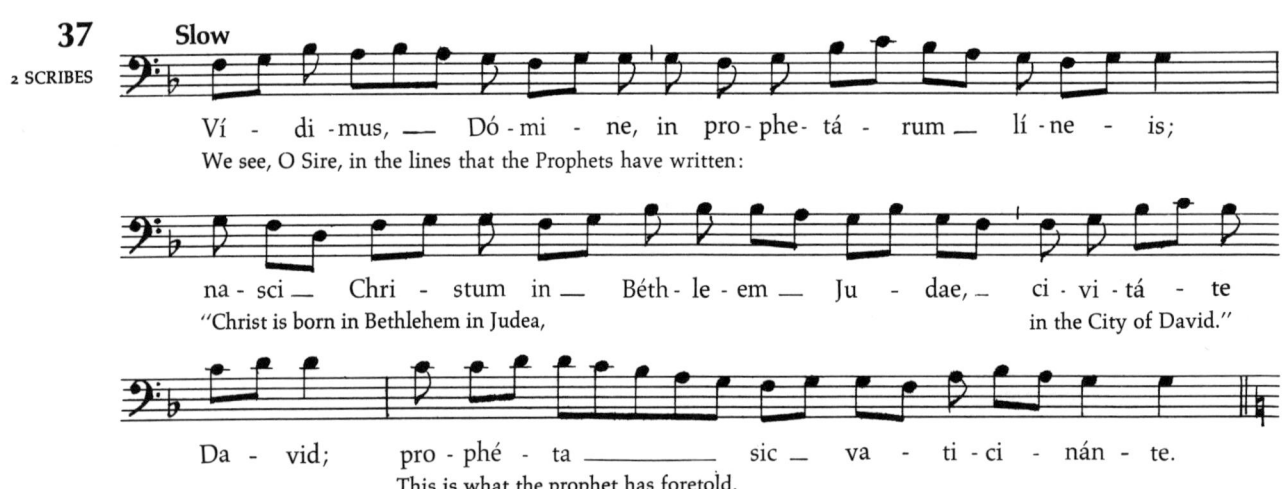

Ví - di - mus, Dó - mi - ne, in pro - phe - tá - rum lí - ne - is;
We see, O Sire, in the lines that the Prophets have written:

na - sci Chri - stum in Béth - le - em Ju - dae, ci - vi - tá - te
"Christ is born in Bethlehem in Judea, *in the City of David."*

Da - vid; pro - phé - ta sic va - ti - ci - nán - te.
This is what the prophet has foretold.

And indicating with a finger let them pass the Book to the incredulous King:

38 **Even slower**
2 SCRIBES

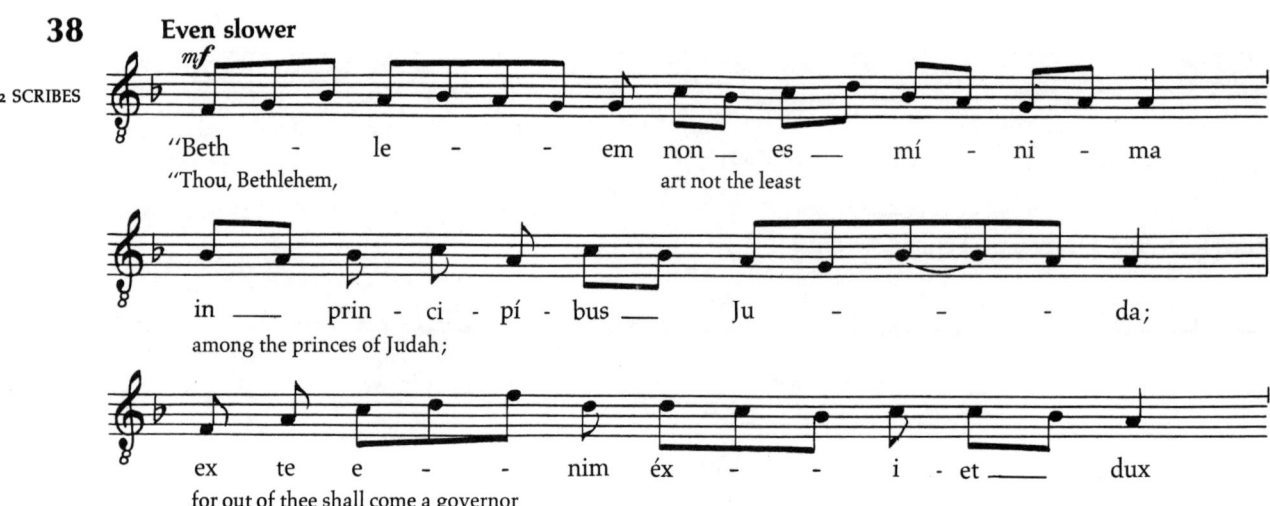

"Beth - le - em non es mí - ni - ma
"Thou, Bethlehem, *art not the least*

in prin - ci - pí - bus Ju - da;
among the princes of Judah;

ex te e - nim éx - i - et dux
for out of thee shall come a governor

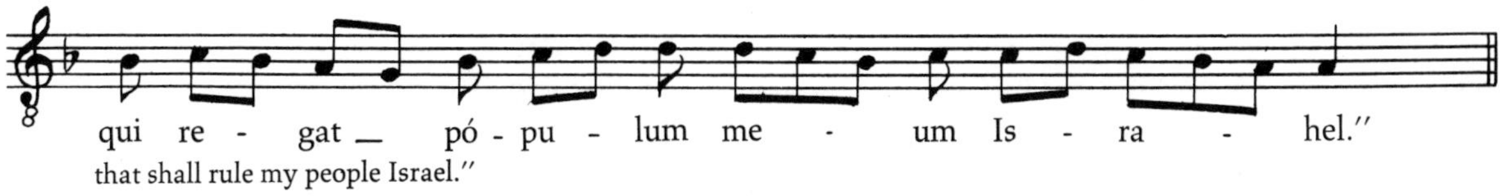
qui re - gat pó - pu - lum me - um Is - ra - hel."
that shall rule my people Israel."

38a

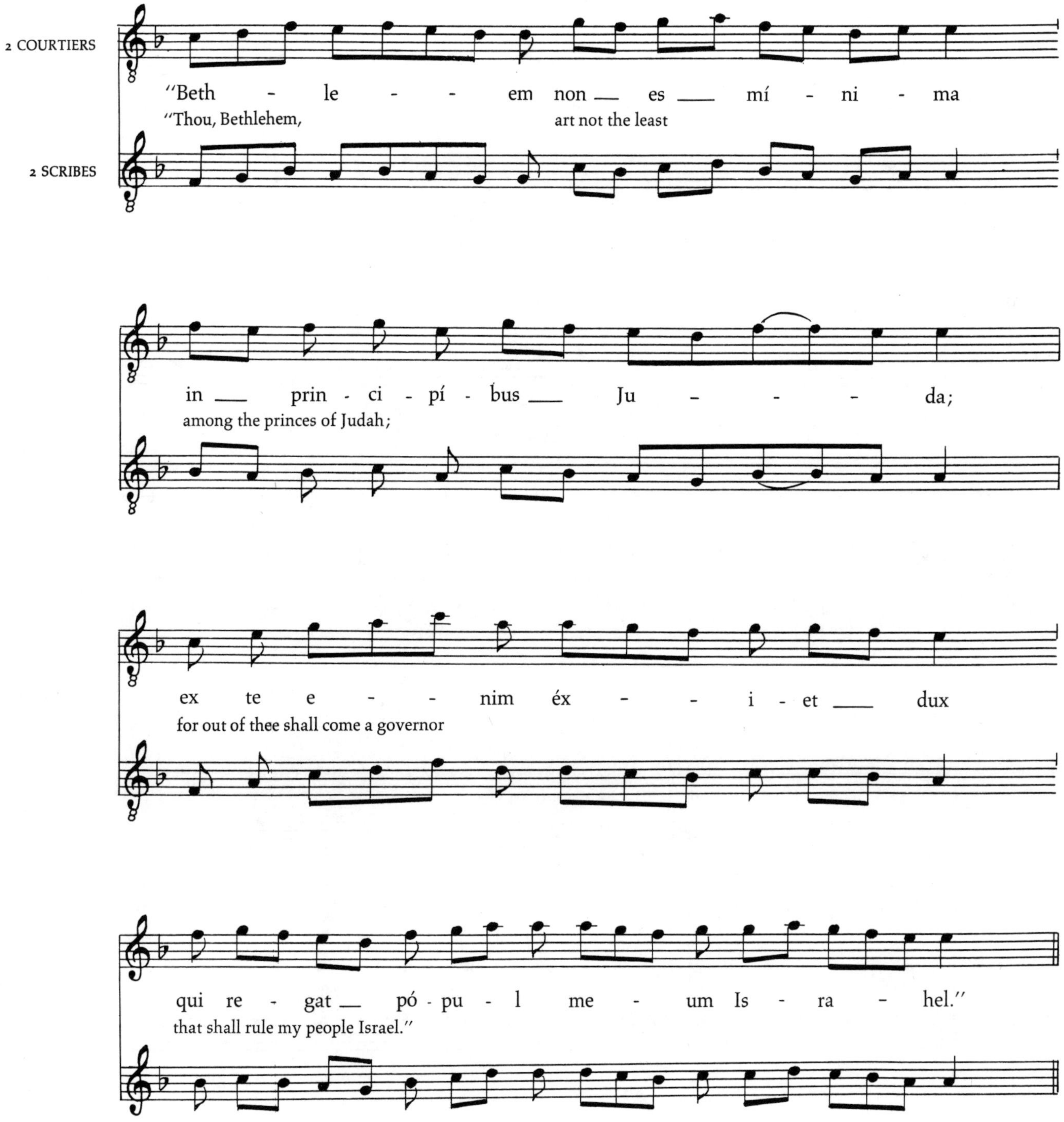
2 COURTIERS
2 SCRIBES
"Beth - le - - em non es mí - ni - ma
"Thou, Bethlehem, art not the least
in prin - ci - pí - bus Ju - - - da;
among the princes of Judah;
ex te e - - nim éx - - i - et dux
for out of thee shall come a governor
qui re - gat pó - pu - l me - um Is - ra - hel."
that shall rule my people Israel."

Then let Herod, having seen the prophecy and inflamed with fury, throw down the Book: but let his Son *(Archelaus)*, hearing the tumult, come forward to pacify his Father and stand there to greet him:

39 **In anger—moderately fast**

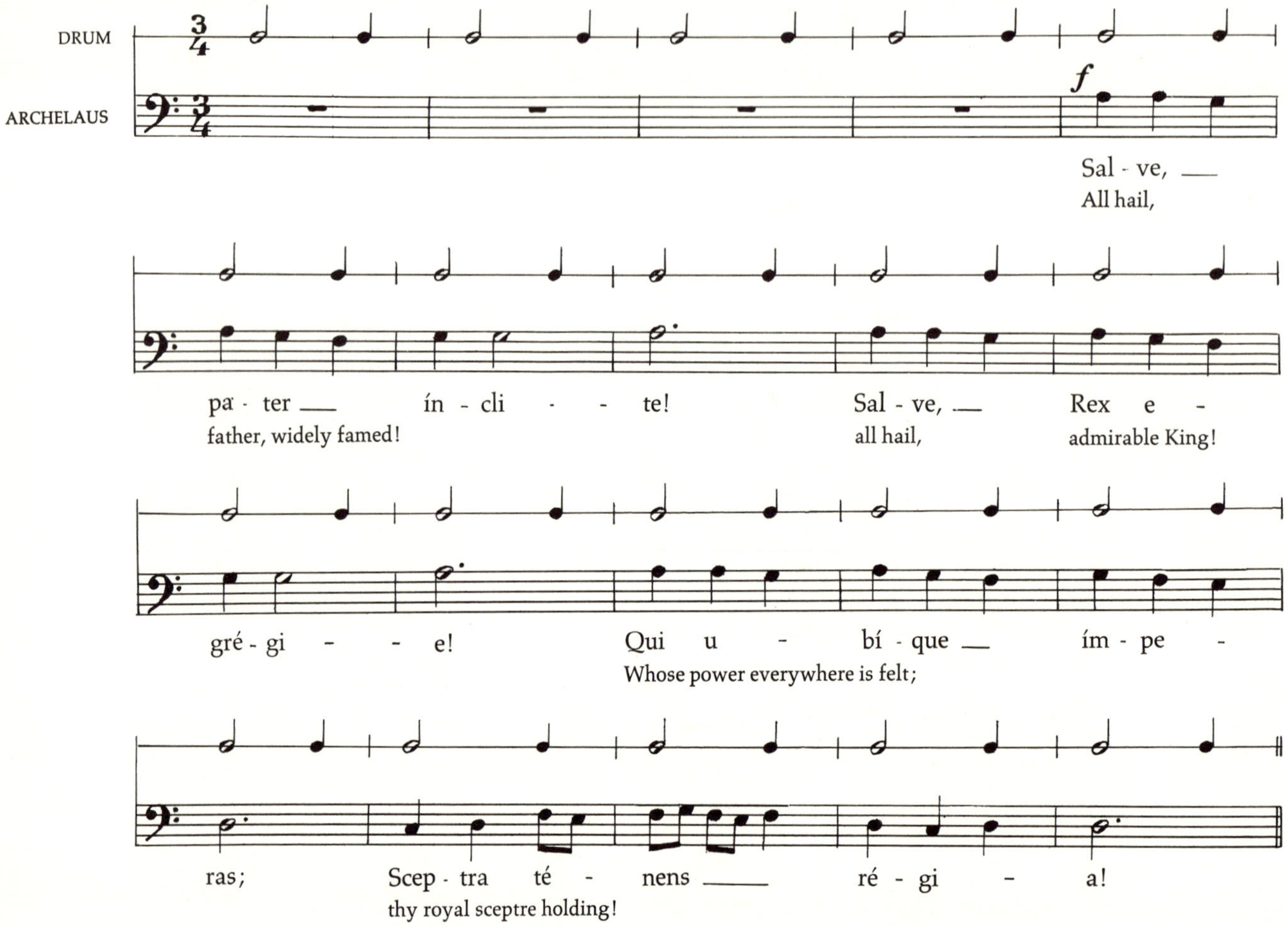
DRUM
ARCHELAUS
f
Sal - ve, —
All hail,
pa - ter — ín - cli - - te!
father, widely famed!
Sal - ve, — Rex e -
all hail, admirable King!
gré - gi - - e!
Qui u - bí - que — ím - pe -
Whose power everywhere is felt;
ras;
Scep - tra té - nens — ré - gi - a!
thy royal sceptre holding!

Herod:

40

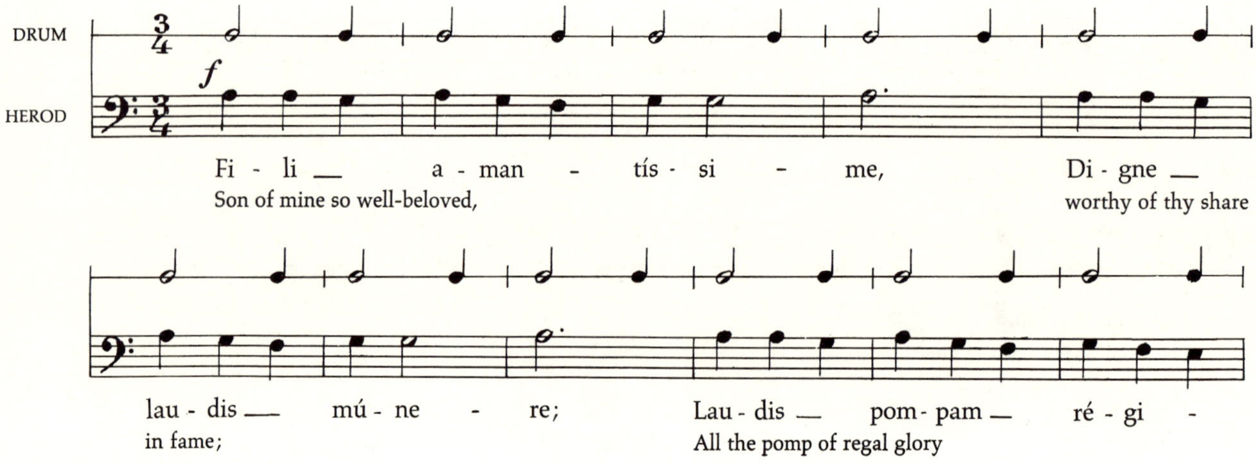
DRUM
HEROD
f
Fi - li — a - man - tís - si - me,
Son of mine so well-beloved,
Di - gne —
worthy of thy share
lau - dis — mú - ne - re;
in fame;
Lau - dis — pom - pam — ré - gi -
All the pomp of regal glory

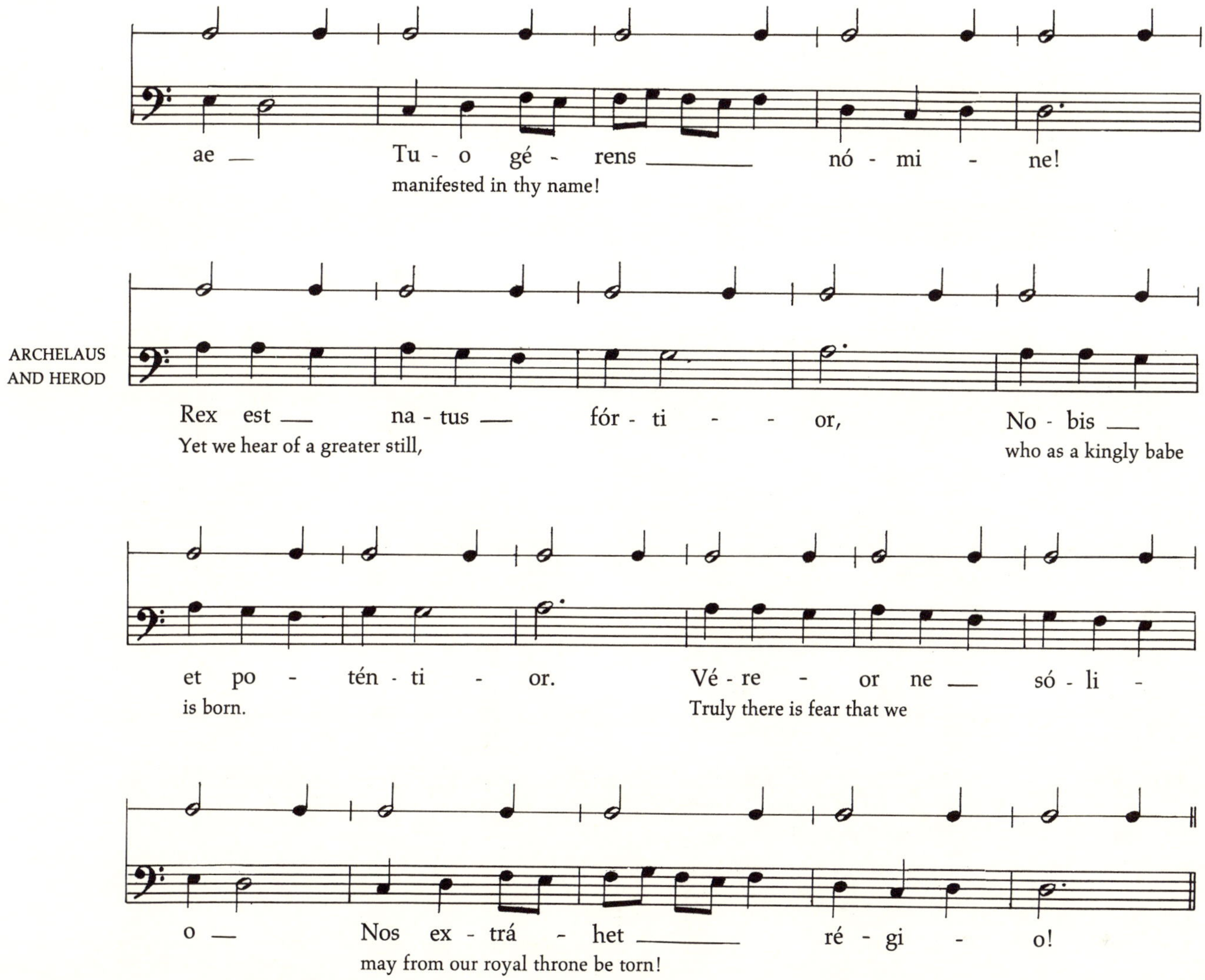

Then let the Son, speaking slightingly of Christ, offer himself as a defender saying:

41

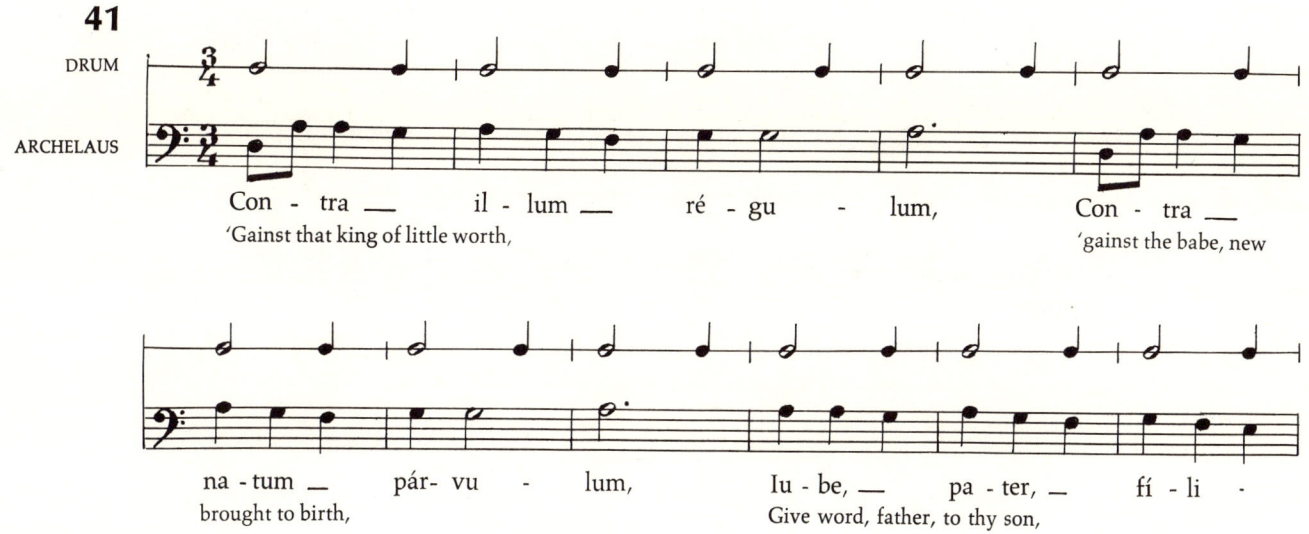

ARCHELAUS AND HEROD

um Hoc in-í-re proe-li-um!
that this war be now begun.

Rex est natus fór-ti-or, No-bis
Yet we hear of a greater still, *who as a kingly babe*
et po-tén-ti-or. Vé-re or ne só-li-
is born. *Truly there is fear that we*
o Nos ex-trá-het ré-gi-o!
may from our royal throne be torn!

Then at last let Herod send away the Magi that they may search for the Child, after vowing homage before them to the new-born King, saying:

42 **Falsely**
mp

HEROD

I - - te, et de pú-e-ro di-li-gén - - ter
Go forth, *and with the utmost diligence make search for the new-born child;*
in-ves-ti-gá - - te; et in-vén - to,
and finding him,
re-de-ún - tes mi-hi re-nun-ci-á - te,
return to us again bringing word of him,
ut et e-go vé-ni-ens a-dó-rem e-um.
so that we also may come to offer homage.

42a

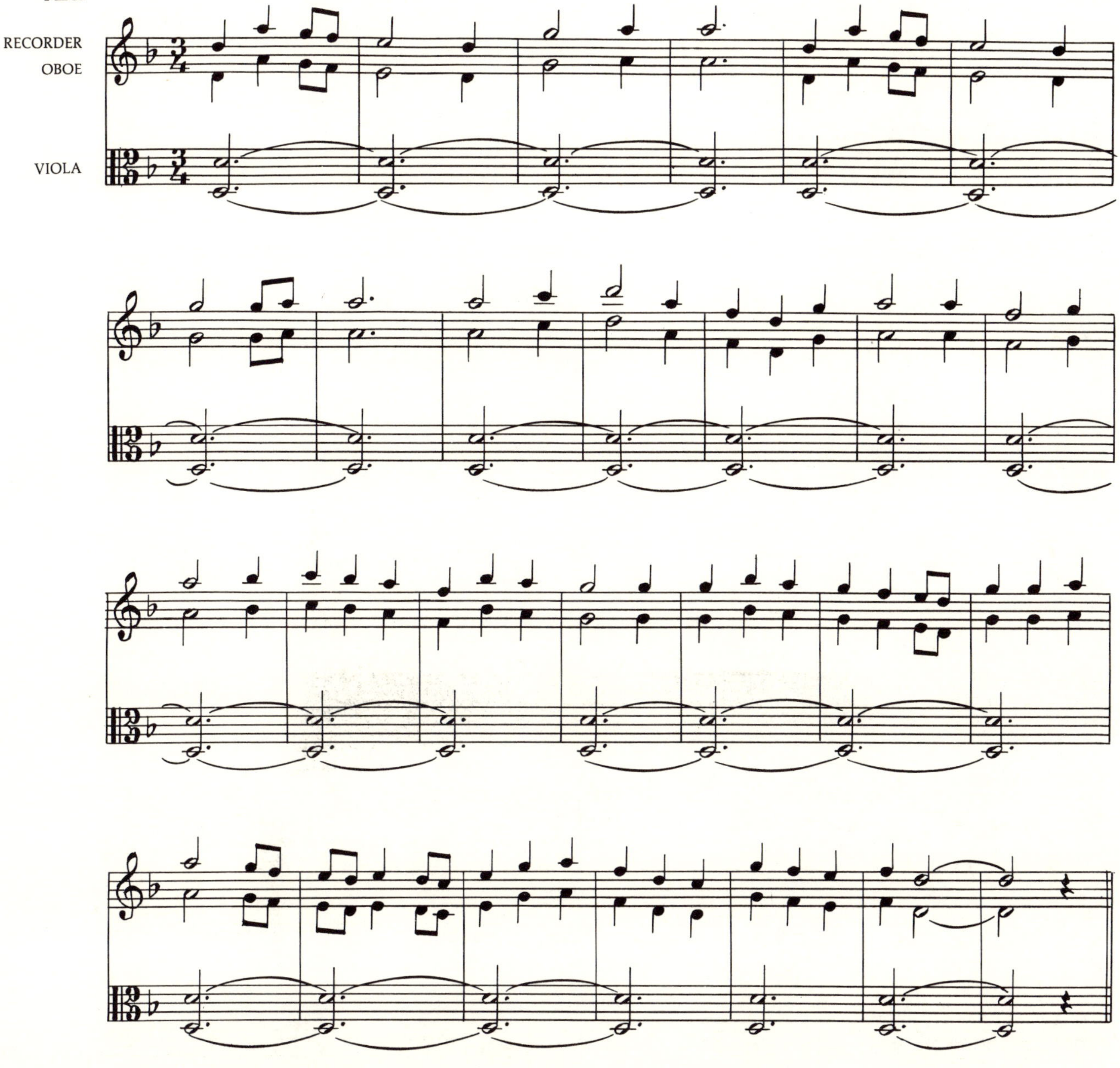
RECORDER
OBOE
VIOLA

As the Magi are going out, let the Star, which has not yet been perceived by Herod, go on before them. Let them point it out to each other as they go. After seeing it, let Herod and his Son threaten it with their swords:

As they play, the Kings, their Musicians and Bearers leave the court and move to down-stage left. Herod's court leaves from up-stage right.

42b

Playfully and fast (in one)

RECORDER
ALL

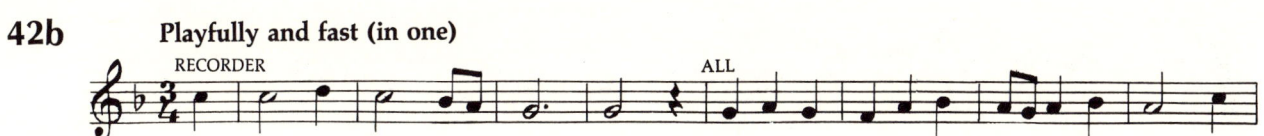

SCENE IV ADORATION OF THE MAGI

Magi:

43 **Gracefully**

3 KINGS

Ec - ce _ Stel - la in o - ri - én - te _ prae - ví - da,
Lo! The Star in the East already espied,

I - te - rum prae - cé - dit nos lú - ci - da!
Shining brightly,, still doth remain our guide!

Meanwhile let the Shepherds returning from the Manger come along with rejoicing and singing:

44

SHEPHERDS

O _ re - gem _ cae - - - li, _
O, King of Heaven,

Add Angel Choir

SHEPHERDS AND ANGEL CHOIR

cu - i - tá - li - a _ fa - mu - lán -
to whom service is given in all obedience.

tur _ ob - - sé - qui - a! _

Stá - bu - lo _ pó - ni - tur _
He who unites the world is laid in a stable;

qui cón - ti - net _ mun - - dum; _

ia - cet in _ prae - sé - pi - o, _
he is lying in a manger

et in nú - bi - bus ___ to - nat. ___
and yet thunders in the clouds!

To whom the Magi:

45 **Slowly**

3 KINGS

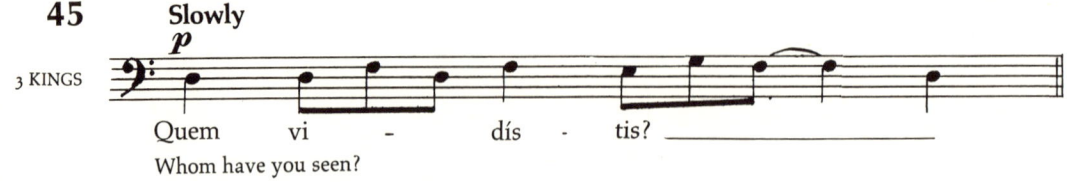

Quem vi - dís - tis?
Whom have you seen?

As they sing the following song, the Shepherds walk into the nave and up the center aisle. If the length of the nave requires it, let them repeat No. 46 until they disappear.

Shepherds:

46 **Innocently**

SHEPHERDS

Se - cún - dum ___ quod ___ di - ctum
In accordance ___ with what was told to us by the Angel

est no - bis ab An - ge - lo ___ de pú - e - ro i - sto, ___
concerning this Child,

in - vé - ni - mus ín - fan - tem pan - nis in - vo - lú - tum,
we found the new-born infant wrapped in swaddling clothes,

Et ___ pó - si - tum ___ in ___ prae - sé - pi - o ___
and lying in a manger

in ___ mé - di - o du - um ___ a - ni - má - li - um. ___
between two animals.

After the Shepherds have gone, let the Magi follow the Star as far as the Manger singing:

47 Joyously

Quem non práe-va-lent pro-pri-a ma-gni-tú-di-ne
He whom neither the earth nor heaven nor the rolling main

Coe-lum, ter-ra at-que má-ri-a la-ta cá-pe-re,
Could, within their widespread boundaries, manage to contain,

lam re - splen - dens fúl - gi - da!

Then let the Midwives, seeing the Magi, say to each other:

48 **Gently**
mp
MIDWIVES

Qui sunt hi - i qui, stel - la du - ce, nos a - de - un - tes in - au - dí - ta fe - runt?
Who are these who, led by a star, advance towards us carrying strange burdens?

The Magi:

49
3 KINGS

Nos su - mus quos cér - ni - tis, re - ges Thar - sis, et Á - ra - bum, et Sa - ba, do - na fe - rén - tes Chri - sto na - to, Re - gi, Dó - mi - no,
We whom you see here are the Kings of Tarsus, and Araby, and Saba, bearing their gifts to the new-born Christ, the King, the Lord,

The Midwives, showing the Boy:

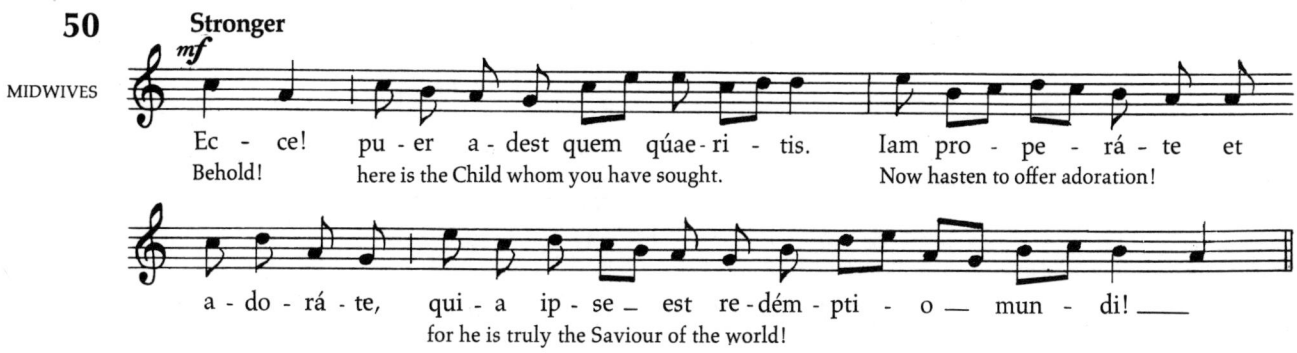

The Midwives slowly open the Manger curtain and close it at the end of the motet.

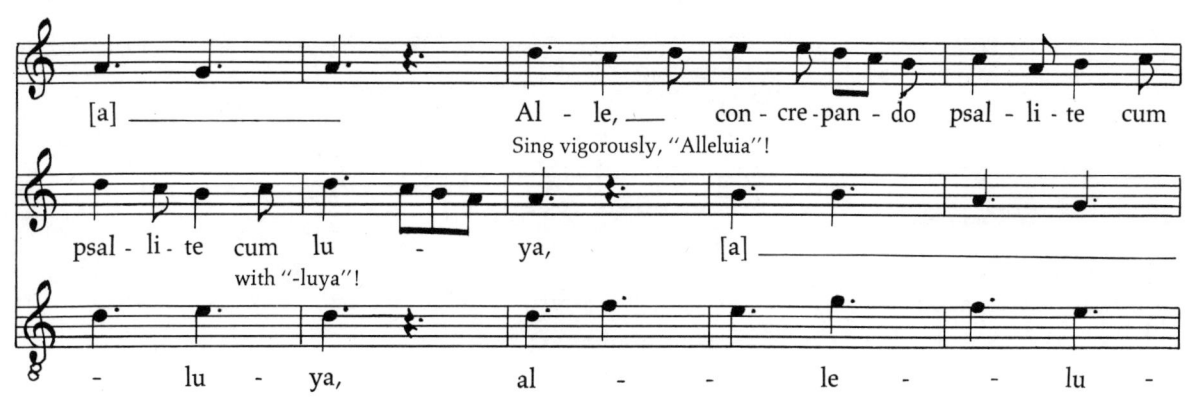

The Magi:

51 Broadly

Sal - ve, Rex sae-cu-ló-rum!
All hail, King of the Ages!

Sal - ve Deus de-ó-rum!
All hail, God above all gods!

Sal - ve, Sa-lus mor-tu-ó-rum!
All hail, Saviour of the dead!

Then let the Magi, prostrating themselves, adore the Boy and make their offerings. The First will say:

52

Sús - ci - pe, Rex, au - rum,
Accept, O King, gold,

Re - gis si - gnum.
emblem of a King.

The Second:

Sús - ci - pe myr - rham, si -
Accept myrrh, emblem of burial.

The Third:

2nd KING: Súscipe thus, tu vere Deus!
Accept incense, O thou very God!

During the following interlude the Three Kings lie down before the Manger and the Midwives place a coverlet over them.

52a

BELLS

All this being done, let the Magi fall asleep, there before the Manger, while an Angel appearing from above warns them in their dreams to return to their own land by another road.

Let the Angel say:

53

ARCHANGEL: Impléta sunt ómnia quae prophétice scripta sunt. Ite, viam remeán-
Fulfilled are all the things of which the prophets have written. When you are returning take another road;

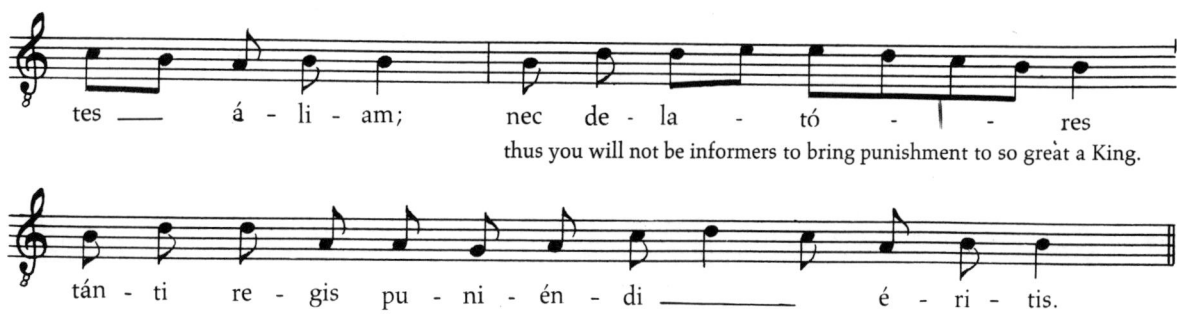

The Magi, having awakened:

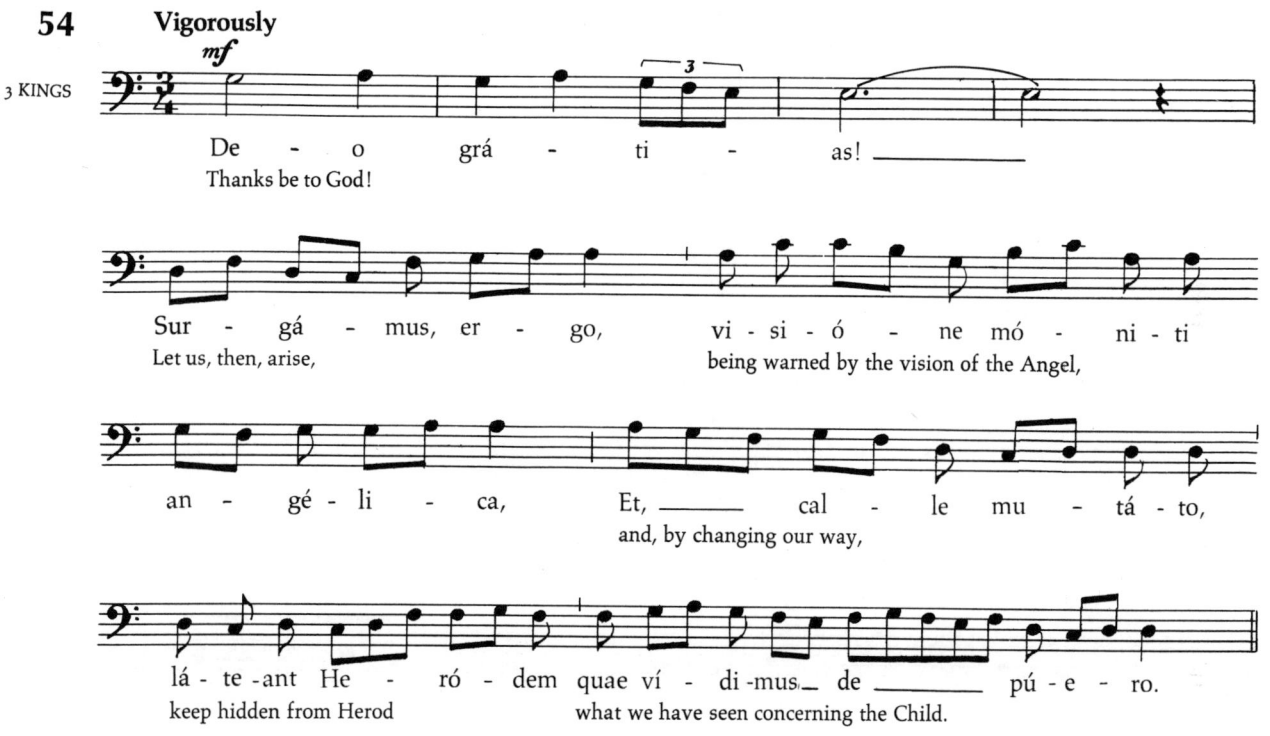

Then let the Magi, departing by another road without Herod seeing them, sing:

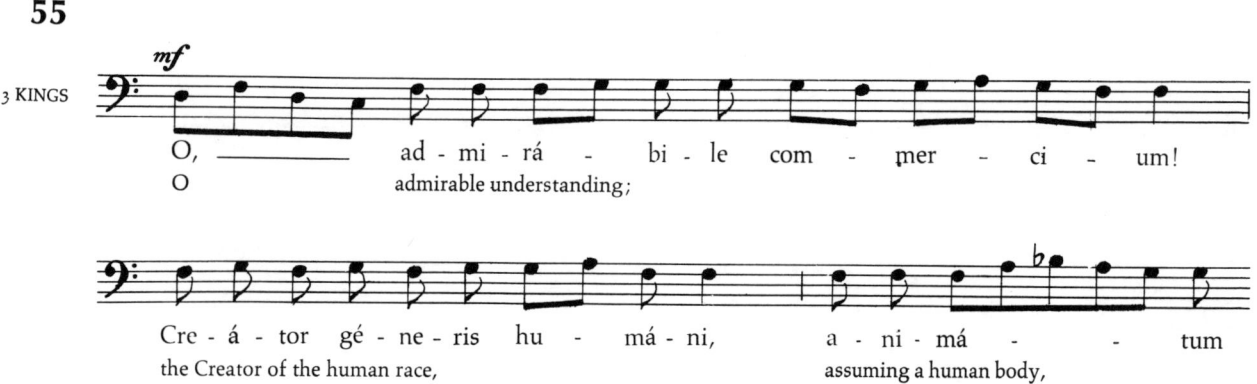

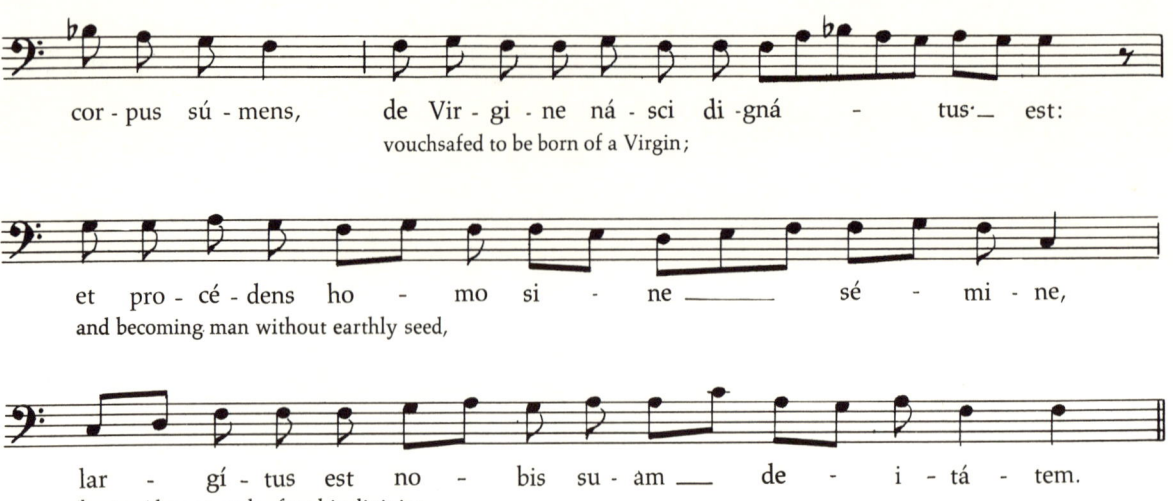

The Magi, led by the Star, process in the chancel as they sing "O admirabile..." and then take their places before the audience in the nave. The Midwives and Angel Choir also begin their recessional.

55a

Singing to the audience:

The Three Kings repeat No. 55 and continue their recessional following the Star down the center aisle to the rear of the nave:

49

II The Slaying of the Children

At the "Slaying of the Children" the Innocents are clothed in white garments and while going joyously about the monastic church they pray to God, thus:

It is here suggested that "O quam gloriosum . . ." first be sung by the Archangel to enable the Innocents to enter the nave and proceed slowly down the center aisle behind a child carrying a medallion (or banner) on a pole depicting a Lamb carrying a cross. Immediately following the Archangel the Children repeat No. 1 joyously.

Then the Lamb, carrying a cross and coming unexpectedly, goes before them hither and thither while those following sing:

The Children follow the Lamb to down-stage left. Herod, his Son, Armiger and his Musician enter throne area from up-stage right.

Meanwhile, a certain Armiger offers to the seated Herod his scepter, saying:

Meanwhile, an Angel appears above the Manger and warns Joseph to flee into Egypt with Mary. The Angel thrice addresses Joseph:

4 **With urgency—3 times**

BELLS

ARCHANGEL

Jó - seph, Jó - seph, Jó - seph, fi - li Da - vid!
Joseph, Joseph, Joseph, son of David!

As the Archangel calls, Joseph enters the chancel and goes to the Manger.

Then he continues:

5

BELLS *Bells continue on this note at random while the Archangel sings.*

ARCHANGEL

Tol - le pú - e - rum et ma - trem e - ius,
Take the young child and also his mother,

et va - de in Ae - gy - ptum,
and seek the land of Egypt,

et es - to i - bi us - que dum di - cam ti - bi.
and in it remain even until I tell thee.

Fu - tú - rum est e - nim ut He - ró - des
For it will come to pass that King Herod himself

quae - rat pú - e - rum ad per - dén - dum e - um.
will seek out the child to destroy him.

Joseph takes Mary and Child out of the Manger and leaves the chancel from stage left as he sings No. 6.

Joseph, unseen by Herod, departs with Mary carrying the Child. He says:

Meanwhile the Armiger first salutes the King and, announcing that the Magi have returned by a different road, says:

7 **Furiously**

ARMIGER: Rex, in aetérnum vive!
O King, live thou for ever!

Delúsus es, Dómine: Magi viam rediérunt áliam!
Thou art deceiv'd, O master; the Magi have returned by another road!

Thereupon Herod, as though he were shattered, seizes a sword and prepares to slay himself, but is prevented from doing so by his attendants and is pacified saying:

8 **Passionately**

HEROD: Incéndium meum ruína restínguam!
My death would extinguish this my burning passion!

Meanwhile, the Innocents, still walking behind the Lamb sing the following:

9 **With motion**

BELLS

CHILDREN: Agno sacrato pro nobis mortificáto splendórem pá-
Unto the Sacred Lamb, Christ who was sacrificed for us, We offer, under that same token of light, The

tris, splen - dó - rem Vir - gi - ni - tá - tis, of - fé - ri - mus
splendour of the Father, the splendour of virginity.

Chri - sto sub si - gno lú - mi - nis is - to. Mul - tis
From the wrath

i - ra mo - dis ut quos in - quí - rit He - ró - dis A -
of Herod, who has sought for us in many ways. We shall be

gno sal - vé - mur, cum Chri - sto con - mo - ri - é - mur.
saved by the Lamb, that we may share in death with Christ.

The tempo of all pieces from #9 to #13a should remain the same

The Armiger, speaking to Herod, makes this suggestion:

10   **Strong**

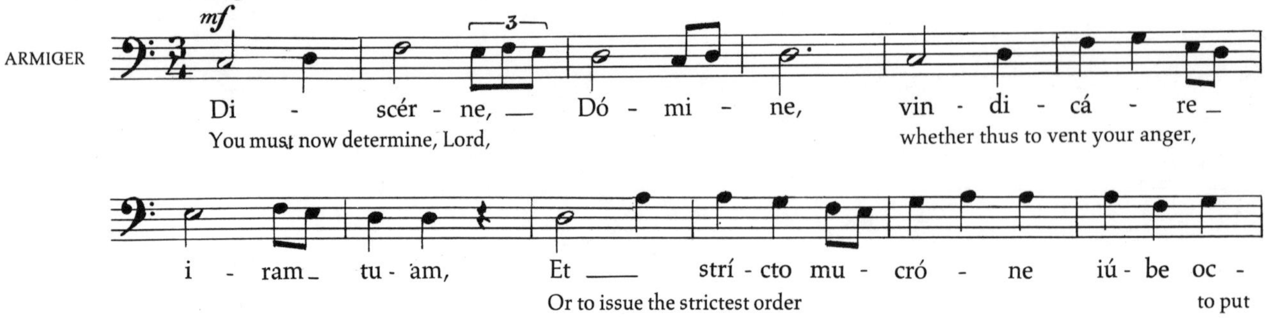

ARMIGER

Di - scér - ne, Dó - mi - ne, vin - di - cá - re
You must now determine, Lord, whether thus to vent your anger,

i - ram tu - am, Et strí - cto mu - cró - ne iú - be oc -
Or to issue the strictest order to put

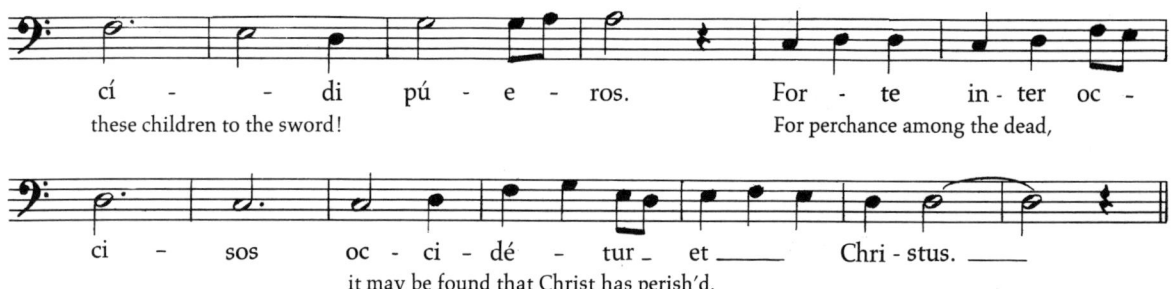

Herod, handing him a sword, says:

Meanwhile, as the slayers approach, the Lamb secretly withdraws and the Innocents acclaim him as he departs.

Here Herod's Soldiers enter, swords held high and join Herod and his court singing:

12a

The Mothers of the victims then intercede with the slayers.

13

O - ré - mus, te - né - rè na - tó - rum pár - ci - te vi - tae! ⎯⎯
We pray you to spare the tender lives of these infants!

13a

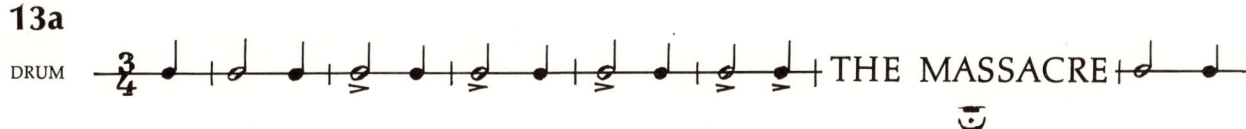

This drum beat continues until the Soldiers and Herod's Musician leave chancel by up-stage right.

Afterwards, when the victims have fallen, an Angel from above addresses them, saying:

14 **A bit slower**

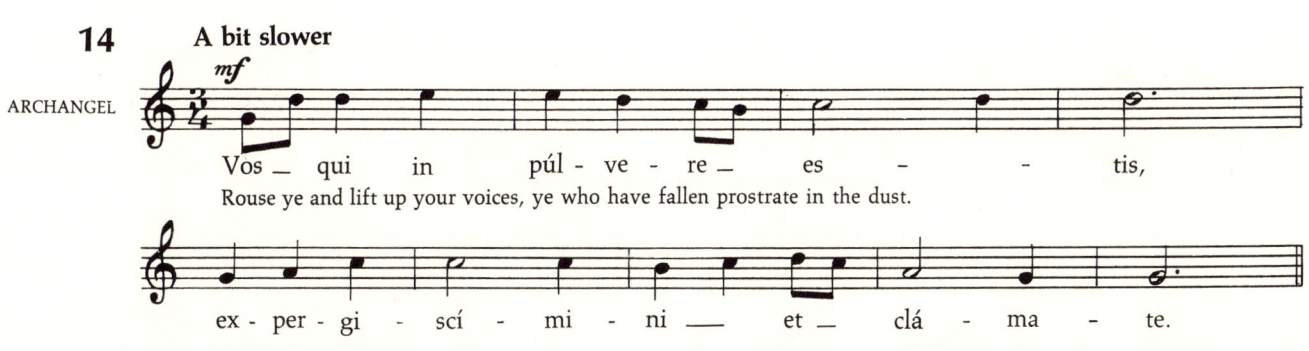

Vos qui in púl - ve - re es - - tis,
Rouse ye and lift up your voices, ye who have fallen prostrate in the dust.

ex - per - gi - scí - mi - ni ⎯ et clá - ma - te.

The prostrate Children:

15

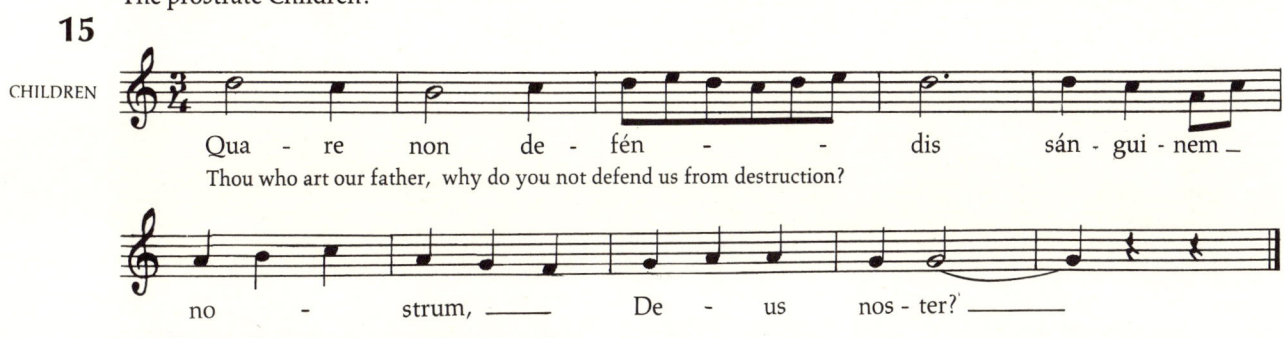

Qua - re non de - fén - - dis sán - gui - nem
Thou who art our father, why do you not defend us from destruction?

no - strum, ⎯⎯ De - us nos - ter? ⎯⎯

It is best perhaps to have one boy sing this.

The Angel:

16

Ad - huc sus - ti - né - te mó - di - cum ⎯ tem - - pus ⎯⎯
Remain here but for a little while,

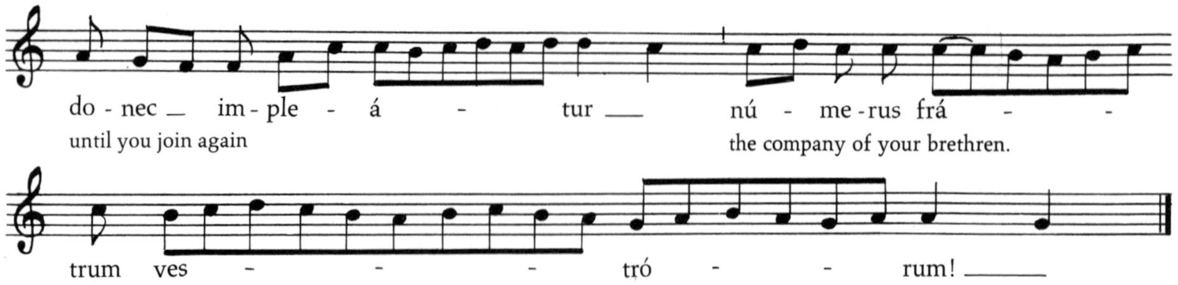
do - nec — im - ple - á - tur — nú - me - rus frá - -
until you join again
the company of your brethren.
trum ves - - - tró - - rum! —

Rachel enters while the Archangel sings.

Rachel is then brought in with two Consolers:
Standing over the Children she laments, sometimes falling, saying:

17 Moderately fast—same tempo continues through #20

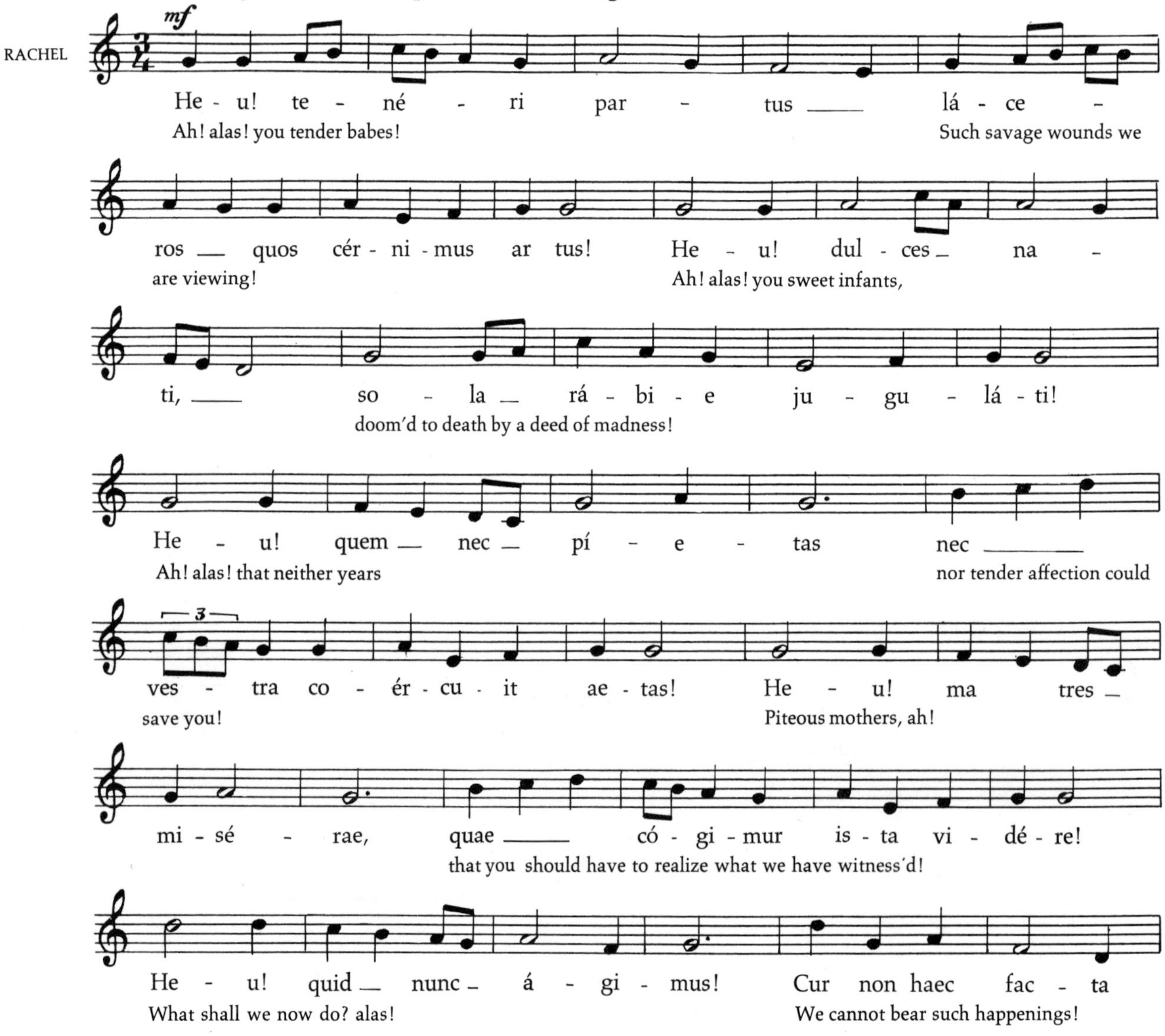
mf
RACHEL
He - u! te - né - ri par - tus — lá - ce -
Ah! alas! you tender babes!
Such savage wounds we
ros — quos cér - ni - mus ar tus! He - u! dul - ces — na -
are viewing!
Ah! alas! you sweet infants,
ti, — so - la — rá - bi - e ju - gu - lá - ti!
doom'd to death by a deed of madness!
He - u! quem — nec — pí - e - tas nec —
Ah! alas! that neither years
nor tender affection could
3
ves - tra co - ér - cu - it ae - tas! He - u! ma tres —
save you!
Piteous mothers, ah!
mi - sé - rae, quae — có - gi - mur is - ta vi - dé - re!
that you should have to realize what we have witness'd!
He - u! quid — nunc — á - gi - mus! Cur non haec fac - ta
What shall we now do? alas!
We cannot bear such happenings!

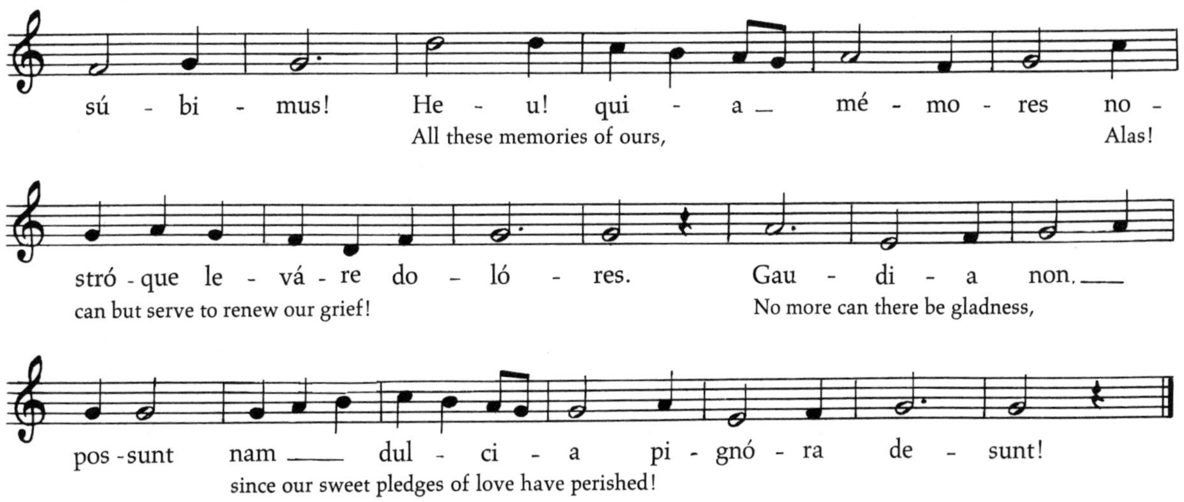

sú - bi - mus! He - u! qui - a mé - mo - res no -
All these memories of ours, Alas!

stró - que le - vá - re do - ló - res. Gau - di - a non
can but serve to renew our grief! No more can there be gladness,

pos - sunt nam dul - ci - a pi - gnó - ra de - sunt!
since our sweet pledges of love have perished!

The Consolers *(Mothers)* support her as she falls, saying:

18

2 CONSOLERS
(2 MOTHERS)

No - li, vir - go Ra - chel, no - li dul -
Do not, O pure Rachel, do not, O sweetest of

cis - si - ma ma - ter, pro ne - ce par -
mothers, Cease weeping in sorrow for the children who

vó - rum fle - tus re - ti - né - re do - ló - rum.
here lie slain.

Si quae tris - tá - ris, ex - úl - ta quae la - cri -
But, as you mourn so, rejoice in the tears you render,

má - ris. Nam - que tu - i na - ti
Since that these your offspring live as the blessed in heaven.

vi - vunt su - per as - tra be - á - ti.

Rachel continues her lament:

19

RACHEL

Heu! heu! heu! Quómodo gaudébo; dum mórtua membra vidébo;
How can I be joyful; forever these mangled limbs seeing;

Dum sic commóta fúero per víscera tota? Me facíent vere púeri síne fine dolére.
When my whole being is so rended by emotion? Truly these sweet children will mean to me perpetual grieving!

O dolor! O patrum mutátaque gáudia matrum ad lugúbres luctus!
Oh, sorrow! Oh, how changed the joy of these parents' devotion Into grief and mourning!

Lacrimárum fúndite fletus, Judaéae florem pátriae lacrimándo dolórem!
Freely let your tears be flowing, Mourning Judea's flow'r, telling of the Fatherland's sorrow!

The Consolers again:

20

5 CONSOLERS / MOTHERS

Quid tu, virgo, mater Rachel,
Why do you weep so, Rachel, mother, lovely in sorrow,
ploras formosa, cuius
You in whose countenance Jacob
vultus Jacob delectat? ce-
doth delight? Even as a
u sororis annicule
baby sister
lippitudo eum
would bring solace to his weary eyes!
iuvat! Terge, mater
Dry your brimming eyes, O mother!
flentes oculos!. Quam te
Rivers of tears do not become your
decent genarum rivuli?
cheek.

Then Rachel:

21

Quickly

RACHEL

Heu, Heu, Heu! Quid me incusástis fletus incássum fudísse?
Wherefore do you say that I have shed these tears so vainly?

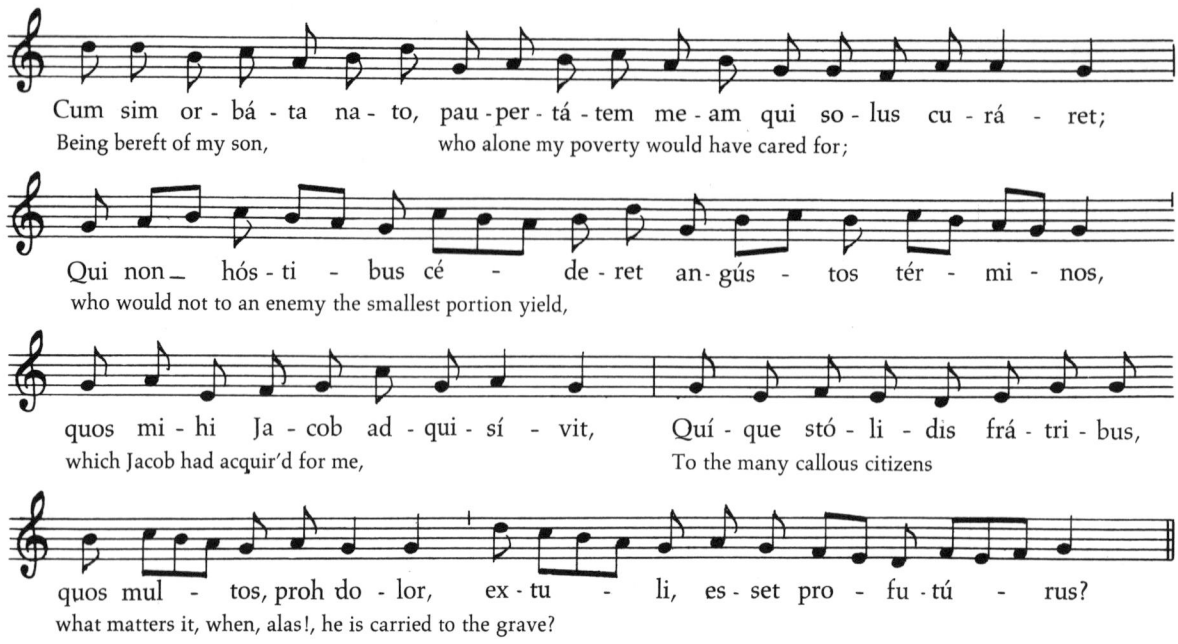

Cum sim or-bá-ta na-to, pau-per-tá-tem me-am qui so-lus cu-rá-ret;
Being bereft of my son, who alone my poverty would have cared for;

Qui non hós-ti-bus cé-de-ret an-gús-tos tér-mi-nos,
who would not to an enemy the smallest portion yield,

quos mi-hi Ja-cob ad-qui-sí-vit, Quí-que stó-li-dis frá-tri-bus,
which Jacob had acquir'd for me, To the many callous citizens

quos mul-tos, proh do-lor, ex-tu-li, es-set pro-fu-tú-rus?
what matters it, when, alas!, he is carried to the grave?

Then the Consolers, lifting the fallen Children, say:

22 **Slower**
p

5 CONSOLERS
MOTHERS

Num quid flen-dus est is-te,
Why must you weep for the child,

qui re-gnum pos-si-det cae-lés-te.
when he has gained a heavenly kingdom?

Quid-que prae-ce fre-qúen-te mí-se-ris
Whatever may be, he will be help'd by the frequent and sorrowful prayers of his brethren?

frá-tri-bus a-pud De-um au-xi-li-é-tur?

Again Rachel, falling upon the Children:

23 **Somewhat slower**
p

RACHEL

An-xi-á-tus est in me spi-ri-tus me-us;
Great is the anguish which possesses my spirit;

in ___ me tur - bá - tum est ___ cor ___ me - um.
within me my heart is troubled.

The Consolers then lead Rachel away and meanwhile an Angel from on high utters the following antiphon:

24 **Quicker**

BELLS

Bells continue on this note at random through No. 24.

ARCHANGEL

Sí - ni - te pár - vu - los ve - ní - re ___ ad me,
Suffer little children to come unto me,

tá - li - um est é - nim ___ re - gnum cae - ló - rum.
for such is the Kingdom of heaven.

The Children rise up at the sound of the Angels' voices, saying as they enter the choir:

The Bell notes are played at random while No. 25 is sung 3 times: the first time by the Children, the second adding Mothers, and finally with Consolers. The Bells should conclude on "G".

25

BELLS

CHILDREN

O ___ Chri - ste,
How numerous, O Christ, is the youthful army of the Father,

quan - tum ___ pa - tri e - xér - ci - tum Iú - ve - nis ___

do - ctus ___ ad bel - la ___ má - xi - ma; ___
vers'd in the great battles:

65

po - pu - lis prae - di - cans, _____ col - li - gis, _____
So much tragedy they proclaim to the people,

um - bras sug - gens cum _ tan - tum _ mi - se - ris.
seeming a gathering of shades.

The Children slowly ascend to their former place as Angels. The slayers and Rachel gather at down-stage left and look toward the Archangel as they sing. The Fleury MS. stage instruction (below) indicates a dumb show for Herod's death and the crowning of Archelaus. Perhaps Armiger should summon two Soldiers to carry the dead King off and then present Archelaus with Herod's crown and scepter.

While this has been going on, Herod has died and in his place Archelaus, his Son, reigns as King. Meanwhile in Egypt, whither Joseph previously fled, an Angel advises him saying:

26

BELLS

ARCHANGEL

Jó - seph, Jó - seph. Jó - seph, fi - li Da - vid!
Joseph, Joseph, Joseph, son of David!

At the sound of the Archangel's call, Joseph and Mary appear and take their place down-stage center.

"g" Bell plays at random while Archangel sings.

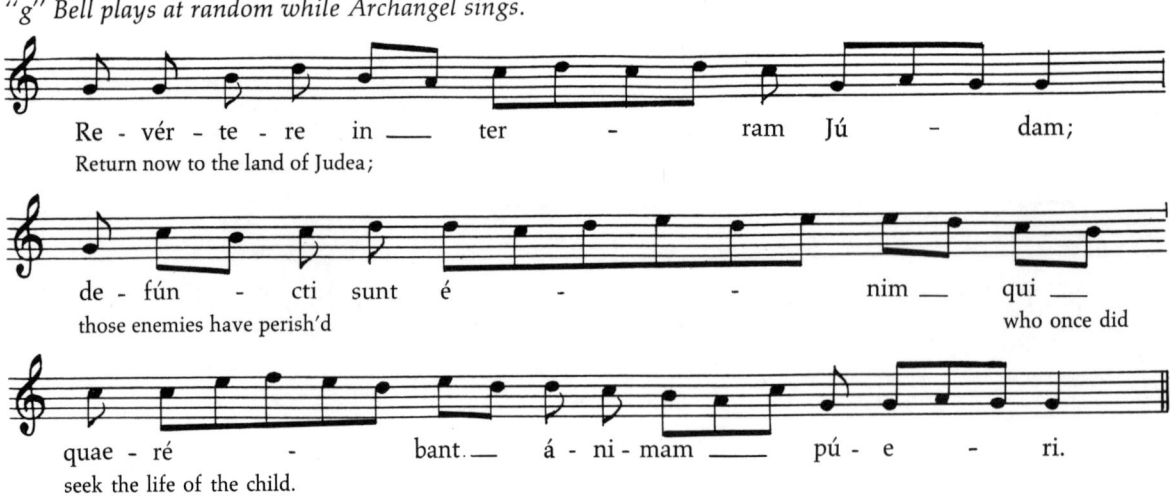

Re - vér - te - re in ___ ter - ram Jú - dam;
Return now to the land of Judea;

de - fún - cti sunt é - - nim _ qui _
those enemies have perish'd   who once did

quae - ré - bant. á - ni - mam _ pú - e - ri.
seek the life of the child.

Thereupon Joseph returns with Mary and the Child, withdrawing into the region of Galilee, saying:

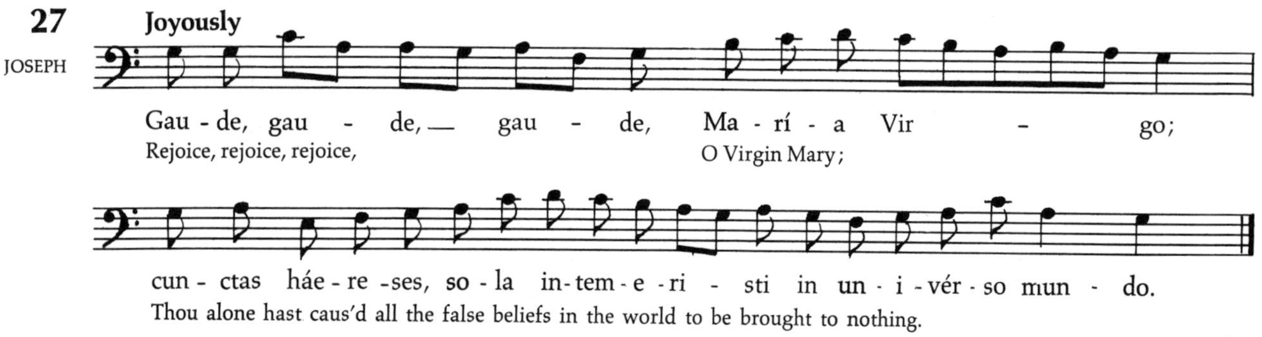

27 **Joyously**

JOSEPH: Gau - de, gau - de, — gau - de, Ma - rí - a Vir - go;
Rejoice, rejoice, rejoice, O Virgin Mary;

cun - ctas hae - re - ses, so - la in - tem - e - ri - sti in un - i - vér - so mun - do.
Thou alone hast caus'd all the false beliefs in the world to be brought to nothing.

The Cantor *(Joseph)* begins Te Deum Laudamus:

BELLS

Bells for the "Te Deum" to be played evenly to the end.

JOSEPH: Te Dé - um lau - da - mus: —

BOYS AND WOMEN: Te — ae - tér - num Pá - trem

MEN: te Dó - mi - num con - fi - té - mur.

o - mnis — tér - ra ve - ne - rá - tur.

Ti - bi ó - mnes An - ge - li,

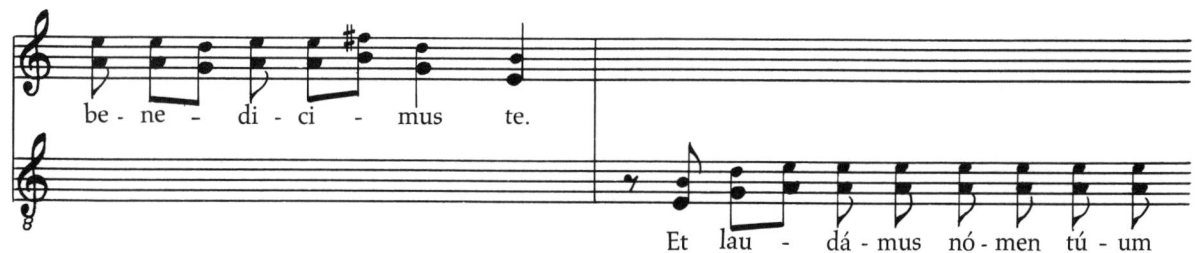

Thus it ends.

Historical Notes

[The material transcribed by W. L. Smoldon from a twelfth-century manuscript, the "Fleury play-book," belonging originally to the monastery of St. Benoît-sur-Loire near Fleury in N. France, and now in the Municipal Library at Orléans (MS 201).]

SOURCES

The rise and full development of the Latin music-dramas of the medieval Church seem to have occupied over three centuries, from the second part of the tenth to the end of the thirteenth.[1] The earliest dramas, emerging from a brief invented dialogue (the "Quem quaeritis" trope) attached to the Introit of the Easter Mass, were concerned with the events at the Sepulchre on the first Easter morning.[2] Dramatic action only became possible when this dialogue was transferred from the Mass to the end of Matins.

Gradually dramas were expanded to include further happenings on Easter Day, and finally later incidents of the Easter season. By the eleventh century other dramas had developed, attached to the Christmas season. The earliest and simplest were concerned with the Gospel story of the Shepherds in the field and at the Manger, and arose similarly from a trope of a Mass—the third of Christmas ("Quem quaeritis in praesepe, pastores?"). Real expansion awaited the development of the story of the Star-led Magi, together with incidents concerning Herod and his court.

About a dozen of the "Magi" dramas survive, of which the one under consideration is perhaps the most attractive. The simplest, an eleventh-century example from Nevers Cathedral (the "Magi" dramas seem to have been a French development), consists of something over a dozen prose items, a mixture of actual antiphons, adaptations of them and other liturgical texts, settings of sentences from the Gospels, together with a certain amount of new invention—words and music. The material as given in the Nevers

---

1. It is important to distinguish the liturgical music-dramas of the Church, *sung* in *Latin* within church walls by clerics, from the later emergence, the mystery-plays, drama *spoken* in the *vernacular* in the open air by secular actors. In the case of the church dramas (to judge by the rubrics) the vocal line seems to have been given only very occasional instrumental assistance, and this from organ and from chime-bells *(cymbala)*. In the case of the mystery-plays the practice of incidental music gave professional instrumentalists ample opportunity to exercise their art.
2. A bilingual acting-version of an Easter Sepulchre drama *(Visitatio Sepulchri)*, associated with the monastery of Fleury and transcribed and edited by the present writer, has been published by the Oxford University Press (London).

version can be thought of as representing a common "core," employed by all the other Magi dramas, with their own individual additions, omissions, adaptations, and versifyings.[3] The Fleury version with which we are dealing is particularly original in dealing with basic material. One of the fullest of the Magi dramas, containing in one shape or another most of the material found in other versions, is that from the cathedral of Freising, and dates from the eleventh century. The development of the type must therefore have been complete by then. With regard to the figures of the three Shepherds, there have survived a few examples, founded on the Christmas trope and the account in St. Luke, II, of a brief and separate *Officium Pastorum*. This shows the Shepherds being informed by the vision of the Angel and journeying to the Manger, where they adore the newborn Child after being questioned by two "Midwives" *(obstetrices)* who, without any Gospel sanction and derived from a second-century tradition, are represented as being present. Most of the Magi dramas make but slight use of the Shepherds, or else ignore them. They are chiefly represented as *returning* from the Manger, meeting and replying to the questing Magi who are on their way to it. Our Magi drama from Fleury, however, gives generous length to the scene of the Angels in the heights and the Shepherds in the field, together with the adoration at the Manger. The incident of the meeting of Magi and Shepherds is made the occasion of two major items by the latter.

The main inspiration for the various incidents in the Epiphany dramas being the second chapter of St. Matthew, it is surprising to find that only three of the surviving examples carry forward the story dramatically to include the Gospel account of the slaying of the young children that was ordered by Herod. The others of the group either end with the escape of the Magi or add some brief sentences which merely reveal Herod's cruel intentions. Of those that stage the massacre, the thirteenth-century Laon manuscript (without music) does indeed include the incident within the framework of a single drama. The playwright-composers of Fleury and Freising, however, chose to develop separate ones, under the headings of *Ad Interfectionem Puerorum . . .* and *Ordo Rachelis*. The second title signalizes the fact that, under the inspiration of St. Matthew II, 17-18, and the prophet Jeremiah, the figure of Rachel is made to be the leader of the mourning mothers. The dramas also include the incident of the Flight into Egypt. Once again it is the Fleury version which handles its material with by far the greatest artistry.[4]

Before considering the two Fleury dramas in detail some note will be taken of the manuscript (the "Fleury play-book") from which they come. As we have already seen, this belonged originally to the Benedictine monastery of St. Benoît-sur-Loire where the two occur successively among a miscellaneous group of ten. As ever, the identity of the creator (or creators) is not known. Although the whole of the dramas were written apparently by a single hand, the individual works vary so much in treatment and quality that one might well conclude that they represented a collection, the units not necessarily originating at the monastery. But the Fleury community was famous during the medieval centuries for its brilliant literary activities, and one can readily believe that it could only have been Fleury that put together the *Ordo ad representandum Herodem*, the *Interfectio Puerorum . . .*, the *Visitatio Sepulchri*, and even the *Pere-*

3. The most important examples are from Compiègne, and from the cathedrals of Freising and Nevers—all these of the eleventh century; from Sicily (Norman-French), Strassburg, Rouen (Montpellier), and from the monasteries of Fleury and Bilsen—all these of the twelfth century. A full-scale version from the cathedral of Laon, of the thirteenth century, shows familiar textual details but no music. In several thirteenth- and fourteenth-century Rouen Cathedral manuscripts the figures of the Magi (as the Three Kings) are associated with the oblation ceremony of the Epiphany Mass. Here, the items characteristic of the Magi dramas are cut down to the level of the Nevers version. It seems difficult to decide whether the Magi type of drama was first inspired by the gift-bearing oblation ceremony contained in the Mass, or that the intrusion of the robed and crowned Kings into the official rite was suggested by the prior existence of such a histrionic form.

4. In considering dramas of the "Slaying" I have disregarded as of small import a brief dramatic scene in verse between Rachel and a consoling Angel, found in an eleventh-twelfth-century Limoges manuscript.

grinus, which are at a much more satisfactory dramatic level than, say, *Tres Clerici*, *Tres Filiae*, or *De Resuscitatione Lazari*. The two "Herod" works, besides representing the best dramatic treatment of their themes, are quite generous in their rubric details as to action. These cast a great deal of light on the manner in which they were first presented. Although perhaps belonging to different feasts ("Magi" at Epiphany—the "Slaying" on Innocents' Day) there can be little objection to staging the two as an entity, since the action is continuous, and as we have seen, there is already one example, a thirteenth-century manuscript from Laon, which definitely blends the two themes in a single drama.

THE PLAY OF HEROD—THE MEDIEVAL PRODUCTION

It must be recalled that these various medieval church-dramas, whether for Easter, Christmas, or saint-day, were intended as religious instruction—designed "to fortify the faith of the unlettered vulgar and of neophytes," as St. Ethelwold's *Regularis Concordia* puts it. The actions took place wholly within church walls, usually between the end of Matins and the concluding Te Deum; sometimes at Vespers; while a few examples actually lead into the Mass itself. The actors were clerics of various grades. There is one instance known of a bishop taking part. Choir boys were used. Lest the modern employment of women be thought of as an anachronism, let it be stated that there is firm evidence as to nuns' being employed (in the parts of the Marys) in what would have been "mixed casts." The present writer readily recalls half a dozen examples, ranging over France, the Germanic countries, Italy, and England. Regarding the matter of dramatic expression, manuscript rubrics often clearly encourage displays of deep feeling. A fourteenth-century *Planctus* at the Cross from Cividale, made up of about a score of stanzas, contains (exceptionally, it is true) close on eighty directions concerned with emotional actions and gestures. As for costuming, in the early stages of the dramas in general there was much adaptation of the ordinary vestments of the sacristy (e.g. albs for angels; dalmatics with amices used as head wrappings, or even copes, for the "women"). Examples of a greater realism are sometimes found in the more developed dramas, concerned with the more important figures. The rubrics of the two Fleury dramas are, however, not very informative on the point. Herod's Courtiers are "dressed as young men," the Scribes are "bearded," the Innocents wear "white garments." No details are given as to how the principals are attired, but in other Magi versions we read of crowns, silken garments, and staves for the Three Kings. However, much other information is given, enabling us to visualize the *mise-en-scène* of the medieval performance in the ample spaces of the monastic church. The Manger, which has survived into modern times as the Christmas Crib, and which, to judge by evidence from other Christmas dramas, was curtained to hide from view the effigies of Mother and Child until the moment of revelation, was situated somewhere in the nave near one of the doors.[5] An important stage property was the Star, apparently a candelabrum, which, again to judge by the rubrics of other dramas, was hung on high and drawn from place to place by means of a cord. In the Fleury rubrics it is first discovered shining above the high altar, and later we are told that it "advances" and "leads" the Magi. "Jerusalem" was apparently a playing space situated in front of the choir doors. Somewhere near at hand, perhaps on some kind of platform, was "Herod's court." Elsewhere, probably a mere space in the nave, was the field of the Shepherds. The Angels, "above," may have appeared in one of the galleries. It must be remembered that the medieval nave was unencumbered by seating, and the space available for action stretched from west end to high altar. Other properties mentioned include the "strange burdens" of the Magi, which prove to be the traditional gifts of gold, frankincense, and myrrh. Also detailed are the swords of Herod and his son, Archelaus, while the latter makes

5. Since in the Fleury version of the "Innocents" Joseph leads Mary to and from "the land of Egypt" she must here probably have been represented by a living person.

reference to his father's sceptre. A "Book of the Prophets" was also needed. In the second drama, the "Innocents," comes the mysterious and symbolic appearance with the children of "a Lamb carrying a cross," who "goes before them hither and thither." How the "Lamb" was originally represented is not made clear. In the present modern performance a large medallion mounted on a tall standard was employed, together with a "standard-bearer." A similar device replaced the potentially risky procedure of a high-suspended and cord-drawn "Star."

THE PLAY OF HEROD—THE TEXTS

A reading of the texts as given in this edition will confirm what has already been said as to the nature of the texts of these Christmas dramas in general. In the main, Fleury uses prose passages, occasionally of some length, but more often in the form of brief dialogue exchanges. In contrast to these are more occasional items in regular rhyming lines of Latin poetry. A number of the longer prose passages, and even some of the shorter ones, are actual liturgical antiphons or other service pieces, relevant to the situation and skilfully adapted. Also there are a couple of phrases that suggest that their inventor was well acquainted with the *Aeneid*. On the whole, however, the numerous interchanges of prose dialogue at Herod's court—the King, Armiger, the other court officials, the Magi—represent free composition. In both dramas the textual borrowings from the Gospel accounts are relatively slight, the most notable being items from the opening Shepherd scene, and, at the court, the prophetic utterance read to Herod.

Regarding items in rhyming verse, there are three such in the "Magi" part of the drama. The first (No. 15—"Caldei sumus . . .") is sung by the Three Kings at their first encounter with Herod's court in the person of Armiger. It may represent a borrowing on Fleury's part, since the stanza occurs also in the eleventh-century Freising manuscript, though with different music. The second is an exchange between Herod and Archelaus (Nos. 39 to 41—"Salve, pater inclyte . . ."). The poem is found also in the "Montpellier" drama of the same century (without music), so Fleury's authorship must remain in doubt. The third (No. 47—"Quem non praevalent . . .") occurs in varied shapes in several other Magi versions, and indeed represents modifications of an ancient liturgical "sequence," a type of composition which was sung chorally and in antiphonal style, each pair of lines having the same melody. To anticipate musical findings I mention here that the Fleury setting is *not* that of the sequence, and seems to be an original one. Besides these three major items, there are occasional rhyming couplets, clearly intended as verse.

In the "Innocents" part of the drama not only is a greater use made of liturgical adaptations (the children, Joseph, Rachel, even Armiger all employ relevant antiphons) but there is a greater proportion of lines in regular poetic rhythm. The skilfully constructed "Agno sacrato . . ." stanza of the Innocents (No. 9) seems to be Fleury's own invention, but the great emotional scene of the drama, Rachel's lament and the intervention of her Consolers, represents a dovetailing of several different elements. Her first rhyming solo (No. 17—"Heu, teneri . . .") has lines found also in the Freising play, but the "Noli, virgo Rachel . . . " (No. 18) occurs elsewhere only in the thirteenth-century Laon manuscript, and the stanza may well be Fleury's own. Rachel's renewed lament continues in the same poetic rhythm, but it is to be noted that two of the lines can be found in the Freising version. With the resumption of the Consolers' chorus a strange new adaptation can be recognized; from "Quid tu, virgo . . ." (No. 20) to the end of No. 22 (". . . Deum auxilietur") the text consists of a tenth-century sequence by the famous monk, Notker of St. Gall. Being of an early type its lines are irregular and it is without rhyme. Again anticipating the discussion of the musical setting, I mention that Fleury supplies its own melody, owing no debt to Notker. Rachel rounds off her scene with a liturgical antiphon (No. 23). This lament section may have sounded like a textual hotchpotch, but in fact the blending is done so skilfully as to make a homogeneous and effective libretto for one of the most remarkable examples of the use of dramatic melody that can be found in medieval times.

THE PLAY OF HEROD—THE MUSIC

As we have previously noted, the music supplied to any medieval church-drama was never more than that of a single line of vocal melody (as in the case of the liturgy). In a number of instances (mostly of the "breviary" type of manuscript) no music at all is given, but there is every reason to believe that the texts were nevertheless sung. Especially in the earlier centuries the musical settings took the form of *neumes*, a notation which gave only the approximate rise and fall of a melody, while indicating the number of notes to a single syllable. Such a system merely *reminded* the trained singer of a passage which he already had had to memorize. This was succeeded by a gradually developing scheme (the ancestor of our own) which, starting with one "pitch" line and progressing to four, fixed definitely the melodic identity of a note. Mensural values remained undefined, in what gradually became the familiar plainchant "square notation."

It happens fortunately that the two Fleury manuscripts have four-line staves for their music, making pitch quite certain except for places where the original scribe has been careless. Of the other "Magi" and "Innocents" dramas mentioned above, only the thirteenth- to fourteenth-century Rouen versions and the Norman-French example from Sicily show fixed pitches. The best that the rest can do is to use unheighted neumes. These however, through their details, make the identity of a melody reasonably certain when compared with the line readings, and confirm what has previously been said regarding a common "pool" of material in the "Magi" scenes. But whatever occasional parallels can be traced in Fleury's musical settings they seem to reflect an original mind and are the most satisfactory and polished among the surviving Christmas drama material.

In all church-drama manuscripts the texts and music are set down in continuous fashion, broken only by the occurrence of rubrics and illuminated capitals. Thus the transcriber, dealing, say, with any Easter or Christmas drama, will find that one of his tasks is to pick out from the prose sentences those which happen to scan and rhyme, and are therefore intended to be recognized as Latin poetry. When he does so he finds that the musical setting also shows a regularity, and often enough repetitions of melodic phrase. The settings of our two dramas use a technique found in most Easter and Christmas dramas of any length. The prose passages of dramatic dialogue are set to a type of free melody not to be distinguished from the style of the short liturgical antiphon,[6] while relief is afforded by the occasional occurrence of stanzas the music of which the transcriber is usually able to resolve into a regular rhythm, trochaic, iambic, or even duple, which can be set down with modern barrings, it being always remembered that the medieval centuries knew of no such notational strait-jackets. Other medieval music-dramas such as Old and New Testament and Saint plays have librettos which are usually in the form of poems of stanza construction, frequently uniform in pattern, their settings capable of being rendered rhythmically throughout. These works, with their stanza tunes often much repeated, are on the whole much less satisfactory dramatically than those using the techniques illustrated by our two Fleury examples, although *Daniel* must be held to be the brilliant exception.

The settings of the dramatic prose passages of our two dramas show not only melodic attractiveness but subtle workings of melodic motifs of a few notes. Such patternings are particularly apparent in the Magi's music, and in that of those who encounter them at Herod's court. A particularly brilliant piece of dramatic recita-

---

6. According to the views of such scholars as Dom Gregory Murray and the late J. W. Vollaerts liturgical chant before about A.D. 1000 was *rhythmic*. Certain "interpretation" signs carried by the neumes of manuscripts belonging to earlier centuries should, they hold, be accepted as indicating a strict system of note-values, one twice the length of the other. As our particular manuscripts belong to a somewhat later and "corrupted" period of the chant and show none of the rhythmic signs I have no alternative but to render the prose settings as "free rhythm," while observing the usual cadence lengthenings.

tive is Rachel's emotional "Heu! . . . Quid me incusastis . . ." (II, No. 21).

Regarding the several genuine and fairly lengthy liturgical antiphons (e.g. "O regem caeli . . .," "O admirabile commercium . . .," "O quam gloriosum . . .," "Aegipte, noli flere, . . .") these retain their service settings,[7] but a number of other prose items which appear to be indistinguishable from them in style are compositions which cannot be traced to liturgical sources. Such for example are the first three items of the first scene, used not only by Fleury but by Rouen and one or two others of the group.

The Play of Herod is certainly outstanding in regard to its poetic items, which, when the rhythms of their settings are interpreted, turn out to have exceptionally charming and expressive melodies. There is no evidence that forbids us to credit Fleury as being the begetter of these. In the matter of mensural interpretations the trochaic "first rhythmic mode" appears to be the usual solution, but the angry stanzas of Herod and his son (I. Nos. 39-41) gain an additional vigour from the iambic "second mode."[8] The high point musically of the whole work is to me the scene of Rachel's Lament (from II, No. 17 onwards). This surely must be reckoned as one of the finest achievements of medieval melodic art. The subtlety of its pattern constructions will well reward close study, and the phrases of Rachel and her Consolers, repeated and varied as they are, are bound together by a constantly recurring and haunting cadence, which first occurs in the pleading phrase of the Mothers, "Oremus tenere natorum parcite vite!"

---

7. One of the trials of a transcriber is to find that a liturgical item, no doubt well known to the original scribe, and to any cleric of the time, is given as an "incipit" (i.e. only the first few words and notes are set down). If, as is often the case, the particular antiphon or responsory or sequence is "obsolete," then a great deal of detective work has often to be undertaken.

8. There are many differences of opinion among scholars regarding the rhythmic interpretations of the melodies of the troubadours and trouvères, which also were set down in no more than plainchant notation. The same problems arise in relation to the settings of the Latin poetry of the church-dramas. In my transcriptions I have tried to choose the rhythms which I thought best suited the scansions and stresses of the Latin.

EDITORIAL ADDITIONS

It will be found that certain of the items have for various practical reasons been given editorial repetitions. Thus, the importance of the figure of Armiger is underlined by his interception and relaying of messages to Herod, and his adding his own weight to the latter's orders. Again, the message of the prophet that is spoken by the Scribe, so deadly for Herod, is repeated in consternation by the whole court. At suitable moments the rhythmic pieces, Nos. 15, 41, and 47 of the first part, are all given repetitions, while during the action of the Slaughter, where nothing vocal occurs in the manuscript, the Mothers repeat their agonized "Oremus tenere . . ." against the Soldiers' savage "Contra illum . . .," Archelaus' declaration of war in No. 41. In this scene also a menacing use is made of an *ostinato* drum-beat. Two choral items have been added. While certain dramas give opportunity for processional entries or opening unison choruses, Fleury has no such provision. Use has therefore been made of the medieval Christmas sequence "Orientis partibus" ("The Prose of the Ass") set to the tune to which it was sung at Sens cathedral. During the solemn moments at the Manger, when the curtains are withdrawn to reveal the Christ-child and his Mother, a thirteenth-century three-part motet, "*Alleluia psallite . . .*," is sung by the Angel Choir.

Regarding musical accompaniments, the evidence for the employment of instruments during the acting of these church-dramas is almost wholly negative. Whatever use of them is made in modern stagings must depend upon the principles of good taste, and the fact that in medieval times the dramas were performed during the Hour services of the church, when a restricted use of organ and of chime-bells only was permitted.

There will be noticed the occasional editorial suggestion as to the use of simple *organum*—the singing of a second part to the given one at the distance of a fifth or fourth, which in the period might have been introduced extempore.

W. L. SMOLDON

The Play of Herod

LITERAL TRANSCRIPTION

The following literal transcription of the pages of the "Fleury play-book" (Orléans MS 201, pp. 205-220) from which *The Play of Herod* in its acting-version form has been derived, sets out the texts and music of the two dramas, as far as possible in accordance with the original, here reproduced alongside. The musical notation is, for the sake of clarity, rendered in "black semibreve" form. The non-specialist will probably find it easier to follow than Gregorian notation. Through the use of slurs it manages still to keep plain the syllabic neume-groupings. Light "linking-notes" (*liquescents*) are indicated by smaller size black notes.

The editorial features, which have been sparingly added, are enclosed in pointed brackets 〈 〉. The items themselves have been separated out, but it will be seen that in the original the scribe used every inch of space in continuous fashion, showing breaks only by illuminated capitals, heavy double bar-lines, and very occasional stops. I have written out in full words that were left abbreviated in the manuscript. Where the scribe has clearly blundered I have reproduced the original, but with due comment, and have made the correction in the acting-version.

Notes on certain features of the transcription are given after its conclusion.

W. L. SMOLDON

⟨ I THE REPRESENTATION OF HEROD⟩

Tunc incipit Ordo ad representandum Herodem.

Parato Herode et ceteris personis, tunc quidam Angelus cum multitudine in excelsis appareat. Quo viso, Pastores perterriti; salus annunciet eis de ceteris adhuc tacentibus:

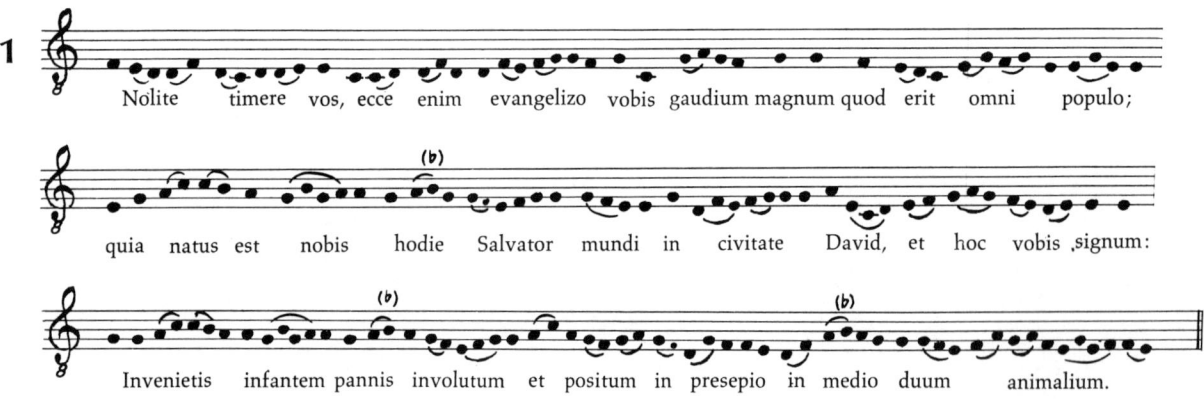

Et subito omnis multitudo cum Angelo dicat:

Tunc demum surgentes cantent intra se *Transeamus*, et cetera:

3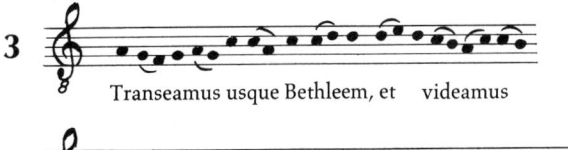
Transeamus usque Bethleem, et videamus

hoc verbum quod factum est, quod fecit Dominus et ostendit nobis.

Et sic procedant usque ad precepe, quod ad januas monasterii paratum erit. Tunc due Mulieres custodientes precepe interrogent Pastores, dicentes:

4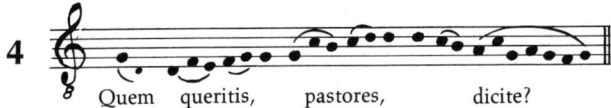
Quem queritis, pastores, dicite?

Respondeant Pastores:

5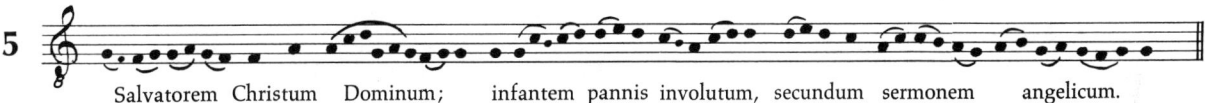
Salvatorem Christum Dominum; infantem pannis involutum, secundum sermonem angelicum.

Mulieres:

6
Adest ⟨hic⟩ parvulus cum Maria matre eius, de qua dudum vaticinando Ysaias propheta

dixerat: "Ecce virgo concipiet et pariet filium."

Tunc Pastores procidentes adorent infantem dicentes:

7
Salve, Rex seculorum.

Postea surgentes invitent populum circumstantem adorandum infantem, dicentes turbis vicinis:

8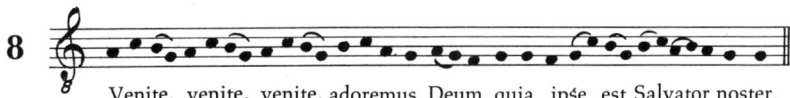
Venite, venite, venite, adoremus Deum, quia ipse est Salvator noster.

Interim Magi prodeuntes, quisquam de angulo suo quasi de regione sua, conveniant ante altare vel ortum Stelle, et dum appropinquant. Primus dicat:

9[1]
Stella fulgore nimio rutilat!

Secundus:

9²
Quem venturum olim propheta signaverat.

Tunc stantes collaterales, dicat dexter ad medium:

10¹
Pax tibi, frater!

Et ille respondeat:

10²
Pax quoque tibi!

Et osculentur sese, sic medius ad sinistrum et sinister ad dextrum. Salutatio cuisque.
Tunc ostendant sibi mutuo ⟨et dicant⟩:

11
Ecce Stella! Ecce Stella! Ecce Stella!

Procedente autem Stella sequentur et ipsi precedentem Stellam, dicentes:

12
Eamus ergo et inquiramus eum, offerentes ei munera: aurum, thus et mirram; Quia scriptum didicimus:

Adorabunt eum omnes reges, omnes gentes servient ei.

prescire venimus quo sit profectus hic vester et unde profectus.

Magi:

21. Regem quesitum duce stella significatum; munere proviso properamus eum venerando.

Oratores reversi ad Herodem:

22. Reges sunt Arabum; cum trino munere; natum querunt infantem, quem monstrant sidera regem.

Herodes mittens Armigerum pro Magis:

23. Ante venire jube, quo possim singula scire qui sunt, cur veniant, quo nos rumore requirant.

Armiger:

24. Quod mandas, citius, Rex inclyte, perficietur.

Armiger ad Magos:

25. Regia vos mandata vocant; non segniter ite.

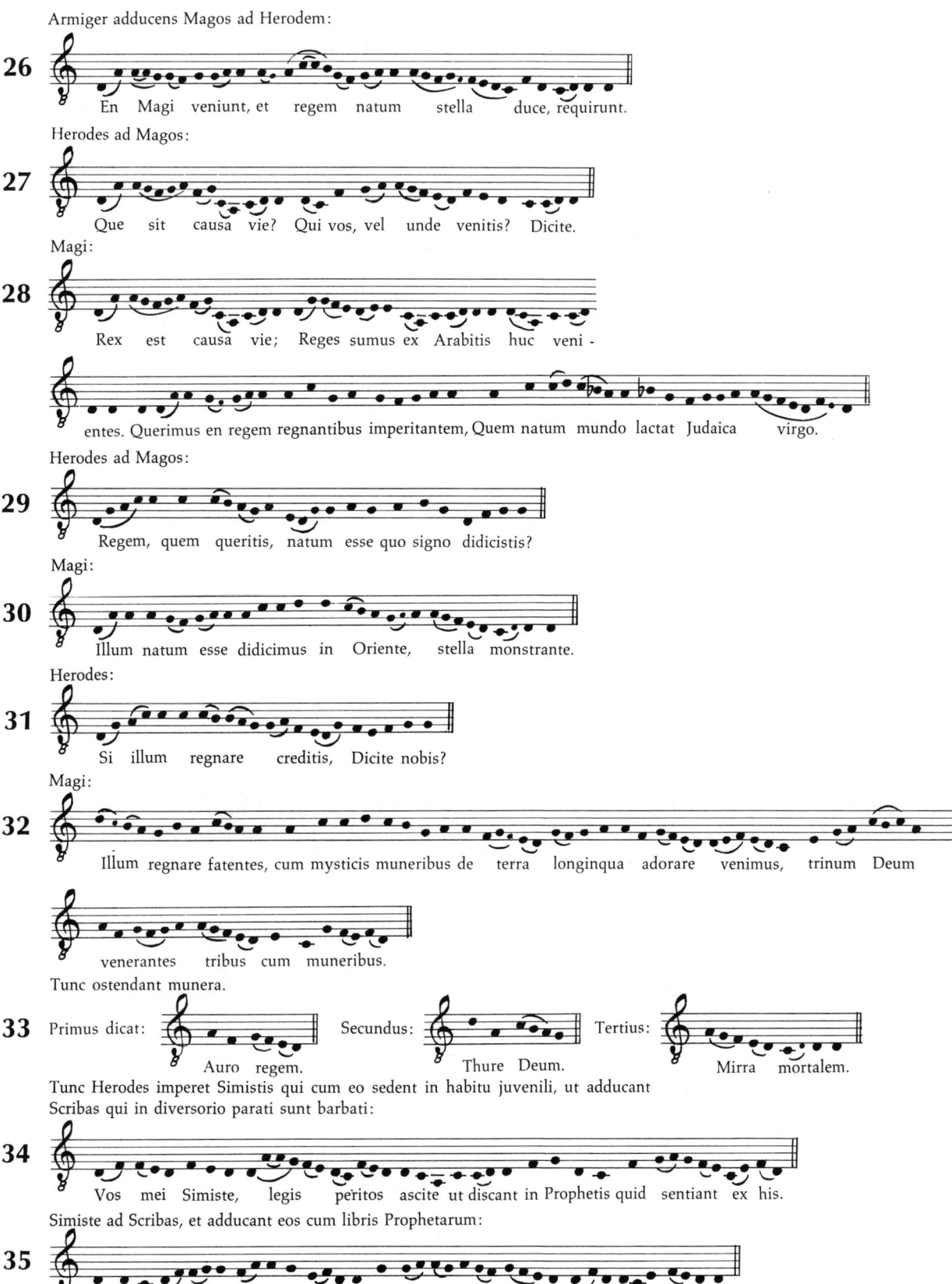

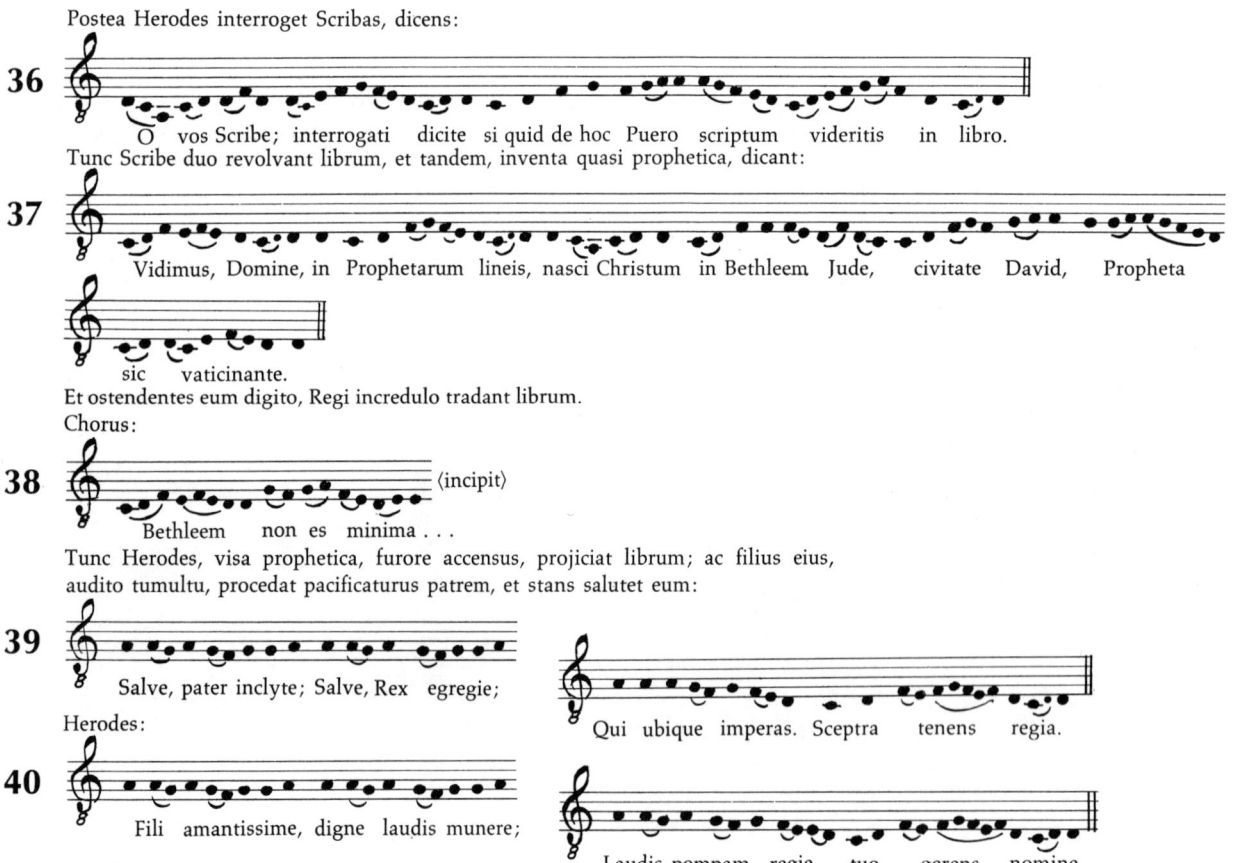

Postea Herodes interroget Scribas, dicens:

36. O vos Scribe; interrogati dicite si quid de hoc Puero scriptum videritis in libro.

Tunc Scribe duo revolvant librum, et tandem, inventa quasi prophetica, dicant:

37. Vidimus, Domine, in Prophetarum lineis, nasci Christum in Bethleem Jude, civitate David, Propheta sic vaticinante.

Et ostendentes eum digito, Regi incredulo tradant librum.
Chorus:

38. ⟨incipit⟩ Bethleem non es minima...

Tunc Herodes, visa prophetica, furore accensus, projiciat librum; ac filius eius, audito tumultu, procedat pacificaturus patrem, et stans salutet eum:

39. Salve, pater inclyte; Salve, Rex egregie; Qui ubique imperas. Sceptra tenens regia.

Herodes:

40. Fili amantissime, digne laudis munere; Laudis pompam regie tuo gerens nomine.

Rex est natus fortior. Nobis et potentior.

Vereor ne solio Nos extrahet regio.

Tunc filius despective loquens de Christo offerat se ad vindictam dicens:

41 Contra illum regulum, contra natum parvulum,

Jube, pater, filium hoc inire prelium.

Tunc demum dimittat Herodes Magos, ut inquirant de Puero, et coram eia spondeat regi nato, dicens:

42 Ite, et de Puero diligenter investigate,

et invento, redeuntes michi renunciate, ut et ego veniens adorem eum.

Magis egredientibus, precedat stella eos, que nondum in conspectu Herodis apparuit. Quam ipsi sibi mutuo ostendentes, procedant. Qua visa, Herodes et filius minentur cum gladiis.

Magi:

43 Ecce Stella in Oriente previsa

iterum precedit nos lucida.

Interim Pastores redeuntes a presepe, veniant gaudentes et cantantes in eundo:

44 O regem celi... ⟨incipit⟩

Ad quos Magi:

45 Quem vidistis?

Pastores:

46 Secundum quod dictum est nobis ab Angelo de Puero isto, invenimus infantem pannis

involutum et positum in presepio in medio duum animalium.

Postea Pastoribus abeuntibus, Magi procedant post stellam usque ad precepe cantantes:

47 Quem non prevalent propria magnitudine

Celum, terra atque maria lata capere,

De virgineo natus utero ponitur in presepio.

Sermo cecinit quem vatidicus stant simul bos et asinus.

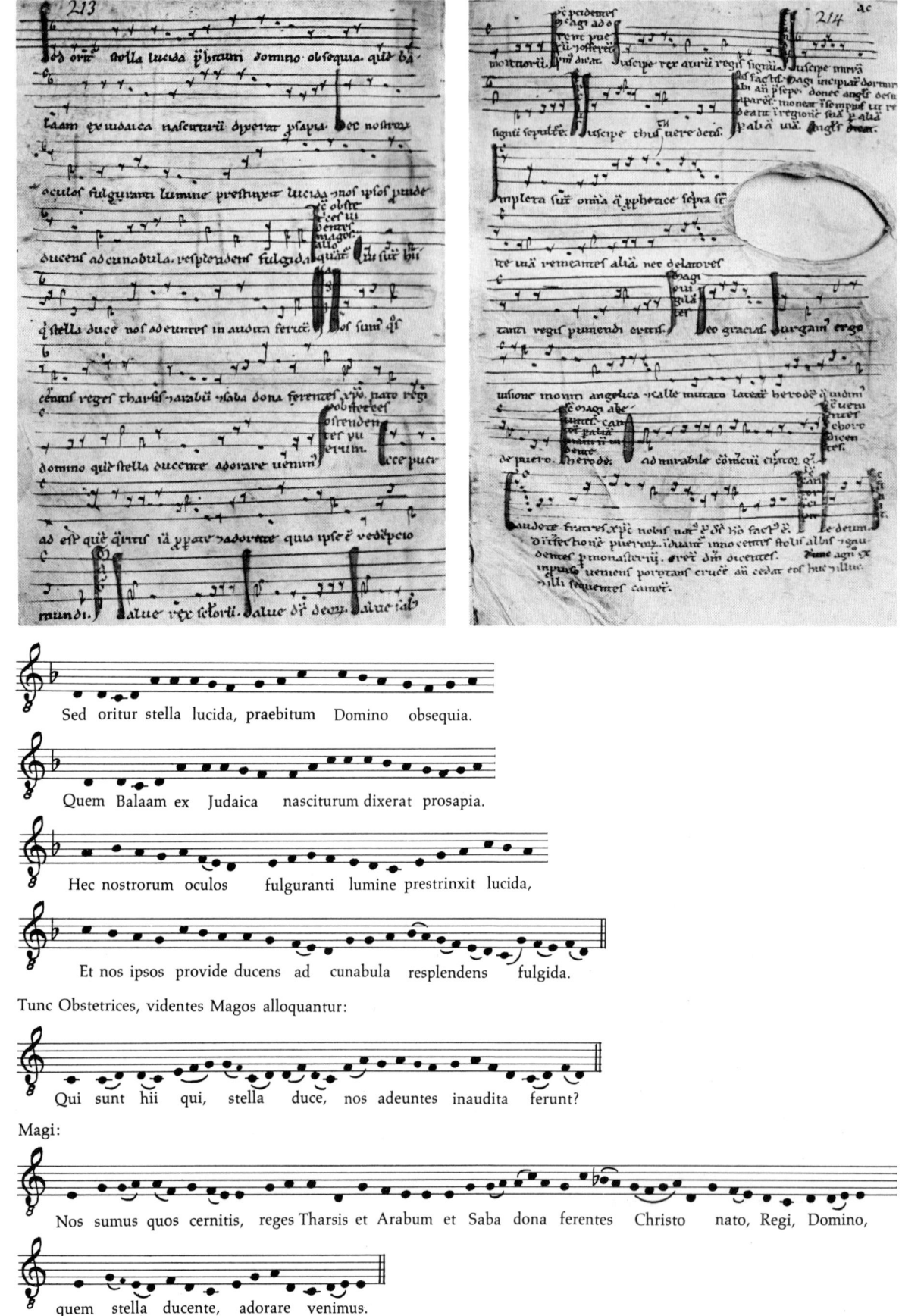

Sed oritur stella lucida, praebitum Domino obsequia.

Quem Balaam ex Judaica nasciturum dixerat prosapia.

Hec nostrorum oculos fulguranti lumine prestrinxit lucida,

Et nos ipsos provide ducens ad cunabula resplendens fulgida.

Tunc Obstetrices, videntes Magos alloquantur:

48 Qui sunt hii qui, stella duce, nos adeuntes inaudita ferunt?

Magi:

49 Nos sumus quos cernitis, reges Tharsis et Arabum et Saba dona ferentes Christo nato, Regi, Domino, quem stella ducente, adorare venimus.

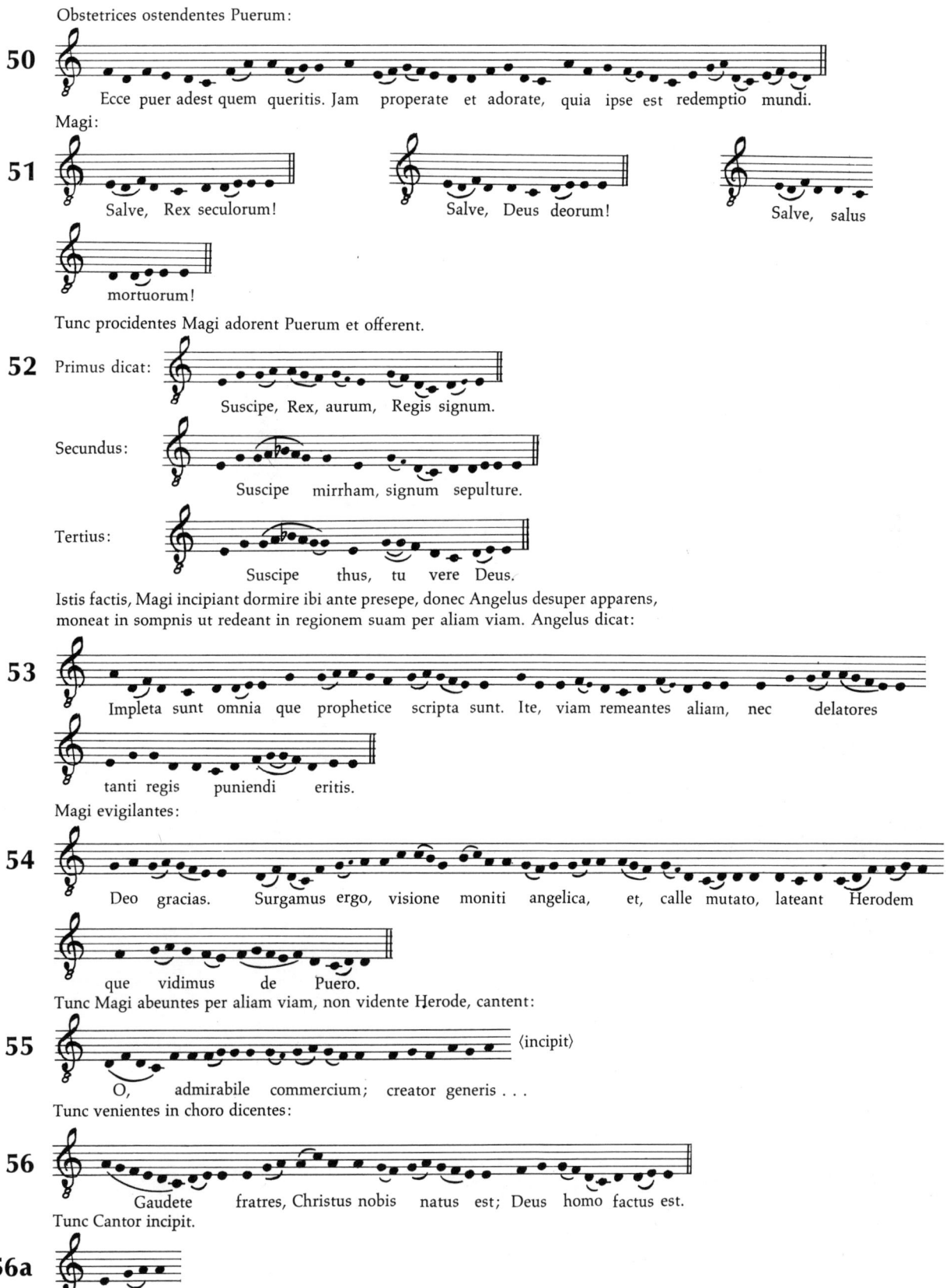

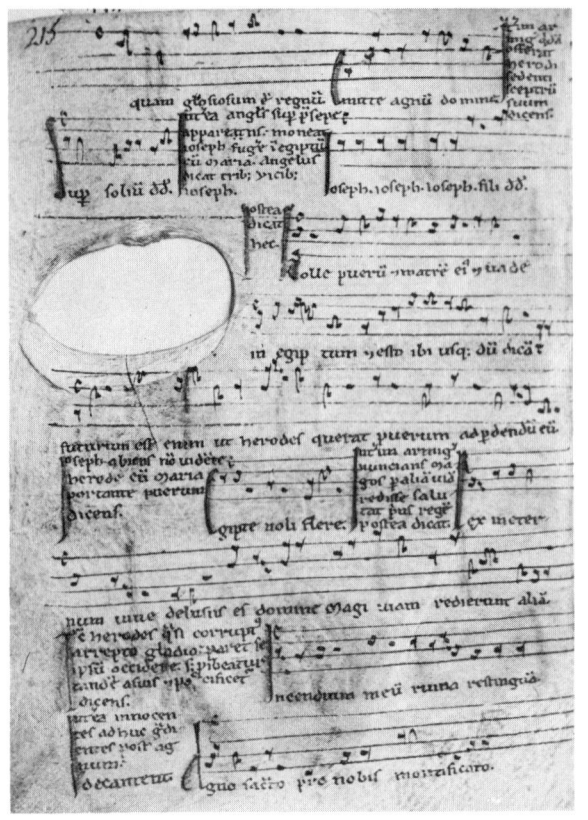

⟨ II THE SLAYING OF THE CHILDREN⟩

⟨A⟩d interfectionem Puerorem induantur Innocentes stolis albis, et gaudentes per monasterium, orent Deum dicentes:

1

⟨O⟩ quam gloriosum   est regnum . . .

Tunc Agnus ex inproviso veniens, portans crucem, antecedat eos huc et illuc, et ille sequentes cantent:

2

Emitte agnum,   Domine . . .

Interim Armiger quidam offerat Herodi sedenti sceptrum suum, dicens:

3

Super   solium   David . . .

Interea Angelus super Presepe apparens moneat Joseph fugere in Egiptum cum Maria. Angelus dicat tribus vicibus *Joseph*:

4

Joseph, Joseph, Joseph, fili David!

Postea dicat hec:

5

Tolle   puerum et matrem eius, et vade in   Egiptum,   et esto   ibi   usque dum dicam tibi.

Futurum est   enim ut   Herodes   querat puerum ad   perdendum   eum.

Joseph abiens, non videte Herode, cum Maria portante Puerum, dicens:

6. ⟨incipit⟩
Egipte, noli flere...

Interim Armiger, nuncians Magos per aliam viam redisse salutat prius Regem; postea dicat:

7. Rex, in eternum vive! Delusus es, Domine; Magi viam redierunt aliam!

Tunc Herodes, quasi corruptus, arrepto gladio, paret seipsum occidere: sed prohibeature tandem a suis et pacificetur, dicens:

8. Incendium meum ruina restinguam.

Interea Innocentes, adhuc gradientes post Agnum, decantent:

9. Agno sacrato pro nobis mortificato,
Offerimus Christo sub signo luminis isto.
Agno salvemur, cum Christo conmoriemur.

Splendorem patris splendorem virginitatis,
Multis ira modis ut quos inquirit Herodis

Armiger suggerat Herodi dicens:

10. Discerne, Domine, vindicare iram tuam,
Forte inter oculos occidetur et Christus.

Et stricto mucrone jube occidi pueros;

Herodes tradens ei gladium dicens:

11. Armiger eximie, pueros fac ense perire.

Interim, occisoribus venientibus, subtrahatur agnus elam, quem abeuntem salutant Innocentes:

12. Salve, Agnus Dei! Salve, qui tollis peccata mundi, alleluia!

Tunc Matres occidentes orent occisos:

13. Oremus, tenere natorum parcite vite.

Postea, jacentibus Infantibus, Angelus ab excelso ut moneant eos, dicens:

14. Vos qui in pulvere estis, expergiscimini et clamate.

Infantes jacentes:

15. Quare, non defendis

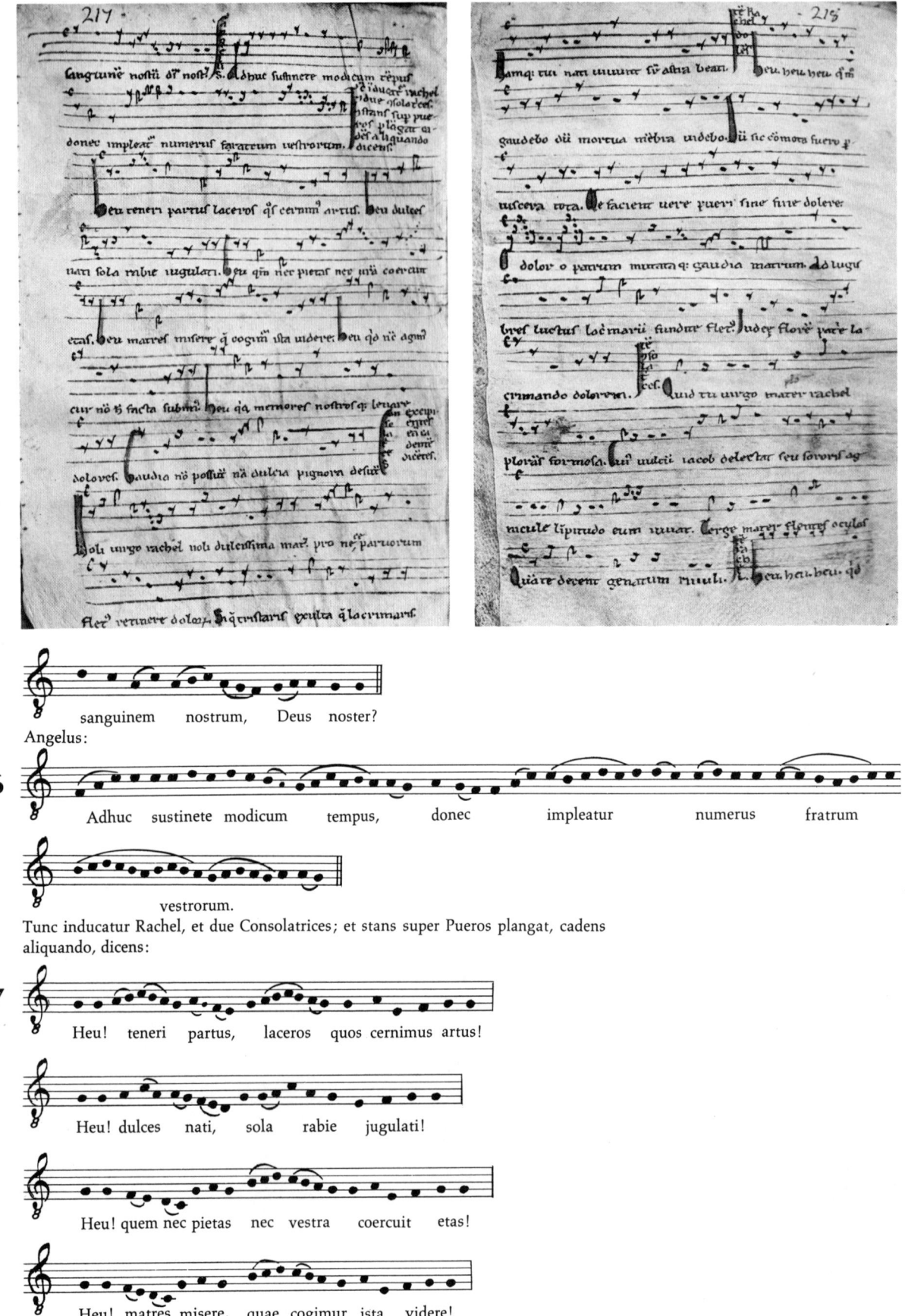

sanguinem nostrum, Deus noster?
Angelus:

16 Adhuc sustinete modicum tempus, donec impleatur numerus fratrum vestrorum.

Tunc inducatur Rachel, et due Consolatrices; et stans super Pueros plangat, cadens aliquando, dicens:

17 Heu! teneri partus, laceros quos cernimus artus!

Heu! dulces nati, sola rabie jugulati!

Heu! quem nec pietas nec vestra coercuit etas!

Heu! matres misere, quae cogimur ista videre!

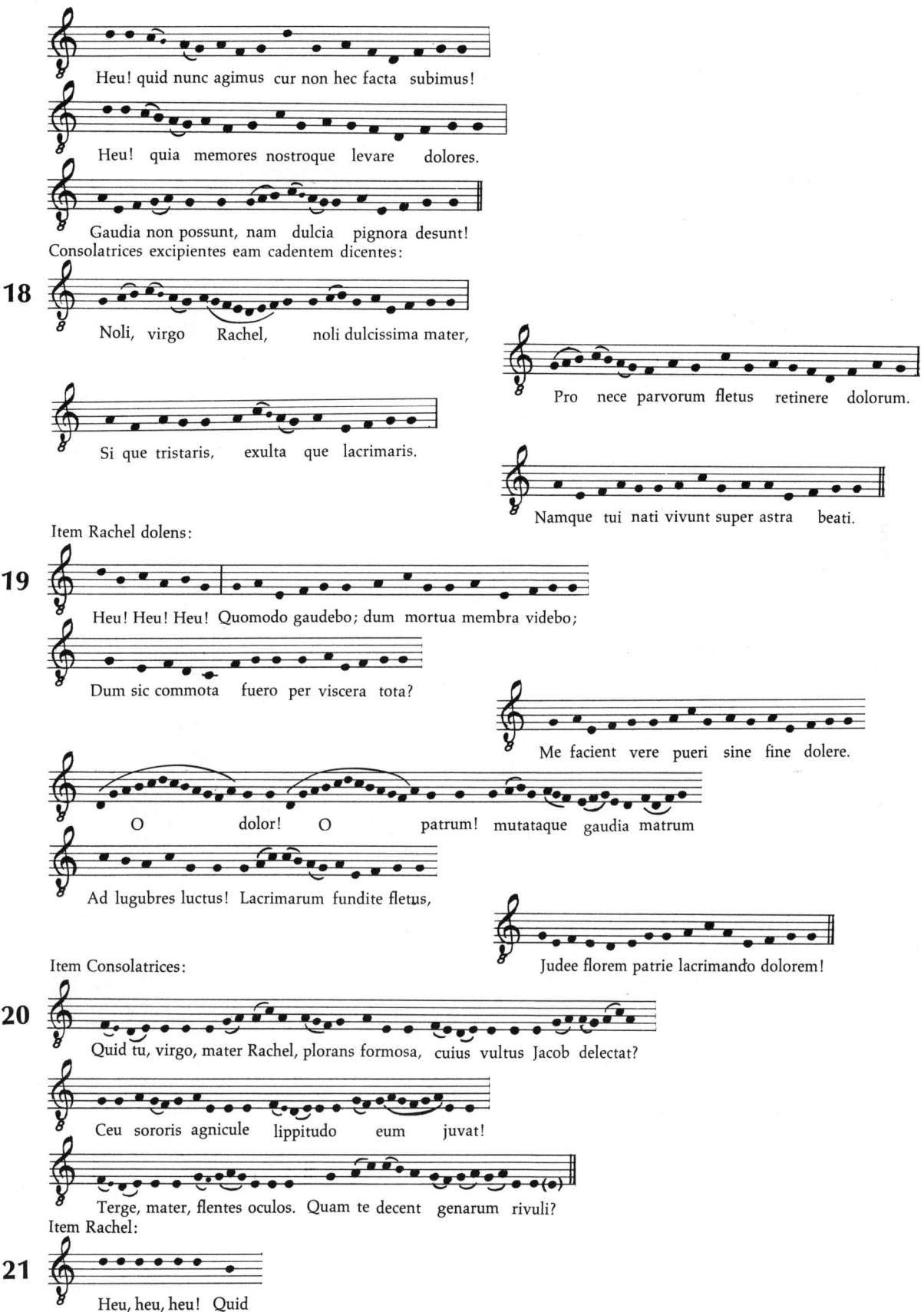

me incusastis fletus incassum fudisse, Cum sim orbata nato, paupertatem meam (qui solus) curaret; qui non hostibus cederet angustos terminos, quos michi Jacob adquisivit, Quique stolidis fratribus, quos multos, proh dolor, extulit, esset profuturus?

Tunc Consolatrices, esupinantes Infantes, dicentes:

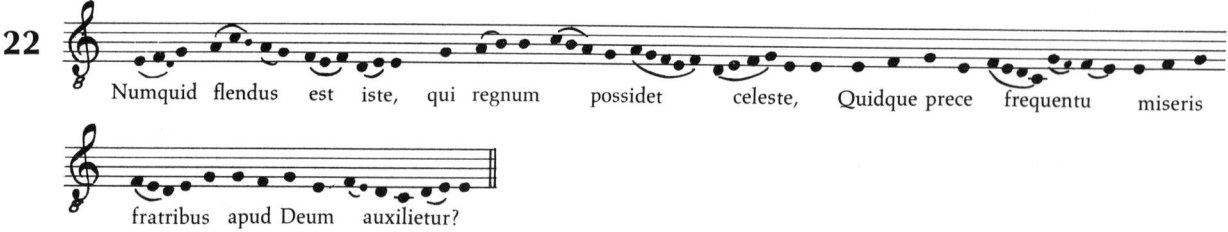

22 Numquid flendus est iste, qui regnum possidet celeste, Quidque prece frequentu miseris fratribus apud Deum auxilietur?

Item Rachel cadens super Pueros:

23 Anxiatus est in me spiritus meus; in me turbatum est cor meum.

Tunc Consolatrices abducant Rachel, et Angelus interim de supernis dicat antiphonam que sequitur:

24
Sinite parvulos . . .

Ad vocem angeli surgentes Pueri intrent chorum dicentes:

25
O Christe, quantum patri exercitum juvenis, doctus ad bella maxima; populis predicans, colligis, umbras suggens cum tantum miseris.

Dum hec fiunt, tollatur Herodes et substituatur in loco eius Filius eius, Archelaus, et exaltetur in regem. Interim Angelus ammoneat Joseph in Egiptum, quo prius secessit, dicens:

26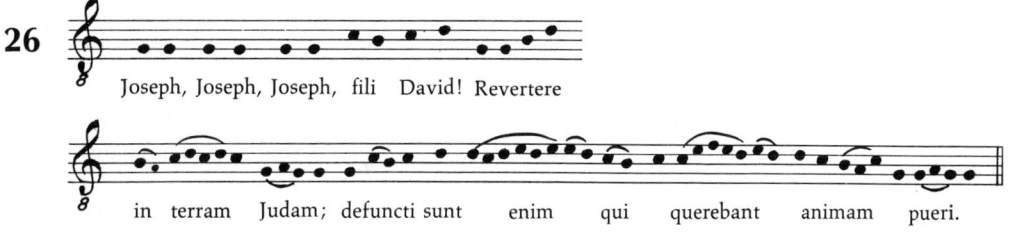
Joseph, Joseph, Joseph, fili David! Revertere in terram Judam; defuncti sunt enim qui querebant animam pueri.

Tunc Joseph revertatur cum Maria et Puero, secedens in partes Galilee dicens:

27
Gaude, gaude, gaude, Maria Virgo; cunctas hereses . . .

Cantor incipit:

27a
Te Deum laudamus . . .

Sic finit.

Notes on the Literal Transcription

⟨THE REPRESENTATION OF HEROD⟩

1 The settings of these Gospel texts seem to be
2 non-liturgical. In No. 1 the manuscript has "natus est *nobis*" instead of the "vobis" of the Vulgate text.

3 This is an ancient Christmas antiphon-setting of the Gospel words.

4 This is a borrowing of the trope of the Introit
5 of the (3rd) Christmas Mass. It is a curious fact
6 that Fleury uses for the first two words ("Quem quaeritis") not the usual music of the trope but that of the Easter "Quem quaeritis . . ." In the acting-version I have, in No. 6, inserted the word "hic" between "Adest" and "parvulus." It is found in all other versions that use the item. I have also put in a clef change that had been overlooked.

11 Regarding the threefold "Ecce Stella," I must confess some doubt as to the actual pitch of the music of the last repetition. If the F clef as written in the manuscript is really intended to be placed in the top *space* of the clef (a position that I have not met with before) then the music as I have given it must for that single phrase be read as being a tone lower. If the clef is meant for the top *line* (again most unusual) then the phrase should be a minor third lower than what I have given, and thus repeating the First King's phrase an octave lower.

8 - I have already commented on Fleury's fine and
42 individual use of certain "pool" items in the Court scene, as well as there being a good deal
(THE of music that appears to be Fleury's own. In the
COURT cases of the two lyrical items (Nos. 15 and 39-
SCENE) 41), the settings of which in my opinion belong to the first and second rhythmic modes respectively, it will be noted that the scribe has actually defined the endings of the lines of the poetry by means of stops. But not consistently. In No. 40 an extra note (an A) seems to have crept in at the word "digne." I believe that the scribe lost count for the moment of his repeated "A's." I cannot credit that the extra A was intended as a *pressus*.

In No. 38 only the beginning of a setting of St. Matthew II, 6 is given—a so-called *incipit*. I have completed text and music from the version found in Madrid, MS 289, fol. 109v.

44 This *incipit* is the beginning of an ancient antiphon, no longer in the Roman liturgy. I have completed it in the acting-version with the kind assistance of the Benedictines of Solesmes. In the Fleury MS. the neumes for the second syllable of "celi" are ambiguous.

46 This reply of the Shepherds is a good example of Fleury's originality, both text and florid free-rhythm setting. They quote to the Magi of the

Angel's first address to them as well as some snatches of his music.

47 This splendid setting of the major part of the text of a liturgical sequence seems to adapt itself to the first rhythmic mode. As I have previously mentioned, the music is not that of the original sequence and may well be Fleury's own. I have, in the acting version (6th line), preferred "praebitura" to "praebitum," adding another C to the melody, as in the line which follows, and which has the same music.

55 This *incipit* belongs to a liturgical antiphon. This time it can easily be completed, since it is still used in the Roman liturgy.

48 In the Magi's oblation scene and the closing
ONWARD stages there is a good deal of use of "pool" material, but with the usual Fleury individuality in regard to melody.

⟨THE SLAYING OF THE CHILDREN⟩

1 This *incipit*, belonging to a liturgical antiphon of Vespers, I have completed from the modern *Antiphonale Romanum*.

2 This *incipit*, belonging to a liturgical antiphon of Lauds, is no longer in the Roman liturgy. I completed it from the Sarum Antiphonal.

3 This *incipit*, belonging to a liturgical antiphon of Lauds, I have completed from the modern *Antiphonale Romanum*.

6 This *incipit*, belonging to a Matins Responsory no longer extant, I have completed from the Sarum Antiphonal. The verse which follows is from Hartker.

9 Although the scribe wrote the rhyming stanza "Agno sacrato . . ." in continuous prose fashion he indicated the line-endings by means of stops and capitals. The music falls readily into the first rhythmic mode.

10 In the third line *oculos* is assumed to be a scribal error for *occisos*. In the matter of textual corrections one can rely on the previous *literary* editing by Karl Young, Du Méril, and others.

14 *Ut moneant* is assumed to be a scribal error
(RUBRIC) for *admoneat*. Incidentally, small errors such as case endings (e.g. *vultum* for *vultus*) have been corrected in the transcription without comment.

17 In the long lyrical rhyming scene between Ra-
ONWARD chel and her Consolers the scribe has again indicated the line-endings of the poetry by means of stops and capitals. The setting is clearly in regular trochaic (first mode) rhythm.

18 It has already been remarked that the Notker sequence text which here commences is not given the original sequence music, but a setting (continued from No. 17) that must surely be Fleury's own.

20 Textual scribal errors have been corrected in the acting-version to *ploras, annicule*, and *lippitudo* respectively.

21 In the setting of this portion of the Notker text there are two notes (a *clivis*) which seem to be going spare. Also, by comparison with other versions of the text, Fleury appears to have left out two words—"qui solus" (three syllables) between "meam" and "curaret." In the acting-version I have inserted them and compromised on their setting. The liquescent of "an*gus*tos" might perhaps be A,B, instead of B,C.

24 I completed this *incipit*, which belongs to an antiphon no longer extant, from Hartker, through the help given me by Solesmes.

27 The text of this *incipit* seems to belong to an antiphon (no longer extant) for the Assumption. But the music is not the same, and none of the Gregorian scholars whom I consulted (even those of Solesmes) could identify it. Finally, Noah Greenberg supplied a version of his own, which kept to the mode and the style of the *incipit*.

W. L. SMOLDON